In Hot Pursuit:

Twelve Things God Wants Us to Pursue

Stephen Olar

In Hot Pursuit

Bibleschooldropout@gmail.com

ISBN-13: 978-0987729231

Bible Studies:

The Bible School Dropout's Bigger and Better Guide to Bible Study - Print and E-book editions available.

The Bible School Dropout's Guide to More Bible Study – Print and E-book editions available

The Bible School Dropout's Guide to Building the Word of God in My Life - Print and E-book editions available

The Bible School Dropout's Guide to Hebrews

The Bible School Dropout's Guide to Dispensationalism

The Bible School Dropout's Book of Charts

The Bible School Dropout's Guide to Genesis 1-11

The Bible School Dropout's Guide to Genesis 12-26

Xtreme Xianity

Novels:

Free – Print and E-book editions available

Icthus – Print and E-book editions available

Table of Contents

The Great Adventure

Welcome to another adventure in our spiritual journey through God's Word.

Often in our Christian walk we wonder and ask: What is God's will for me? Well not me specifically, but if you put your own name… er… you get the picture.

There are many variations of this question as there are answers:

What is God's plan for my life?

Does God want me to become a full time missionary?

How can I understand what God's will is for my life?

What career does God want me to pursue?

Is this what God wants me to do?

You will discover in your spiritual journey those who are not really interested in discovering the answer to these and more questions. Either through ignorance or disobedience they don't want to know what God wants them to do. I am not going to address the willful disobedience issue here, but I can help with those who just don't know what step to take first.

Then there are people like you, who are genuinely interested in wanting to know what God expects you to do. You are hungry to experience God on a whole new level. You are like Daniel as he describes his longing for God in Psalm 42 as a deer seeking to quench her thirst. This book is for you to consider.

Scripture records twelve things God wants us to pursue in our journey. Not just saunter along, stopping to sniff the spiritual roses along the way. It is an all-out race to win the prize.

Paul Wrote in Philippians 3 13-14 "Brethren, I do not count myself to have apprehended; but one thing I do, forgetting those things which are behind and reaching forward to those things which are ahead, I press toward the goal for the prize of the upward call of God in Christ Jesus."

Let's begin our quest to press on towards the mark.

Lesson One

What Does it Mean to Pursue?

When I plan a study one of the questions I consider is where to start it. Some of you may be scratching your head at that statement. After all, don't you start with lesson one and proceed to lesson two then three until the end of the study? Well, yes and no. Yes there is a logical start and sequence the study and the question becomes where to actually start the study.

When putting together this study guide, I create an outline based on some assumption I have to consider. For instance, if I make the assumption all of my readers understand what "pursue" means, then I can skip designing a study and lesson on that particular topic and dive right into the material. It means less work for me and ultimately for you as there is one less lesson to complete.

You may have noticed I made other assumptions in the previous chapters. One of them is not all of you have an understanding of what inductive Bible study is. That leads to the other assumption you have not worked through my Bible study guides which explain the whole thing. As a result there is a crash course section which boils down the essence of the process from two entire books into a few pages. Which mean you are only getting the very basics of what to do and really should backtrack a bit and get yourself a couple of copies for future reference.

For those of you who have read those books, or have an understanding of inductive Bible study then you probably skipped over that chapter.

I also have to make the decision of how much information to supply to you in order to reach the

So in order to get some more depth into this study I made a decision to explore what the Bible has to say about pursuing something or someone. It creates the base and allows us to consider all the possibilities of what God wants us to pursue. So we are officially starting our study dealing with the question: "What does it mean to pursue?"

Let's Take a Look at the Old Testament

Let's start by look up the word "pursue (H7291)." Start filling out the information on your *Word Summary*. For your convenience I have included a list of the references which contain this word. If the reference is listed two or more times, then the word is translated differently. Make a note of the different ways it is translated and used. Unless you are planning on doing an exhaustive study I don't recommend looking up every reference. However that being said, you should look up enough of them to get a good idea how the word is used.

We want to make note of the denotative and connotative meanings. Don't panic... those are fancy words for primary and secondary meanings.

That being said, I am not planning to do this for every lesson. I am only being nice and including it in the first lesson so you have an idea of what to do. For the following lessons I expect you to do your own investigation. K?

What is the basic meaning of this word?

What are some of the other ways this word is used?

Take a look at the first reference of this word.

Complete the *Event* summary. What are the circumstances surrounding the first use of this word?

What did Abraham do to prepare to go after Lot?

What are some other verses which indicate similar circumstances?

When you look at these verses do you see a pattern of intent?

Do you see a pattern of preparation?

Take a look at the following verses:

Psalm 35:6

Psalm 83:15

Jeremiah 29:18

How is the word used in these passages?

How is the word used in Psalm 119:84, 86?

Take a look at Proverbs 21:21 and Isaiah 51:1?

How is the word used in these passages? (Spoiler alert on a future lesson!)

What are the benefits of pursuing righteousness?

Check out how the word is used in Psalm 23:6.

What have you discovered about this word so far in your study?

Now Let's Take a Look in the New Testament

I thing we have looked up enough Old Testament references to give us an idea of how it was used. Now we want to look at New Testament references and discover if the word has similar meaning.

The word we are looking at is G1377. As you work through this study, record your findings on the *Word* summary Chart.

What is the basic Strong's definition for this word?

What do other sources add to this definition?

Take a look at the first use of the word in the New Testament (Matt 5:10-11).

What is the context where this word is used?

How is it used?

What other references use this word in a similar way?

Take a look at Luke 17:23.

What is the context of this passage where this word is used?

How is this word translated here?

What are we not to follow?

How is this word used in Romans 9:30-31?

What is Paul telling the Romans to pursue in Romans 12:13?

Take a look at Philippians 3: 4-14.

Using the *Didactic* Summaries, record Paul's logical arguments.

How does Paul use the word in this passage?

How would you look at Philippians 3:14 differently if it were translated:

"I *follow* towards the mark…"

"I *pursue* the mark…"

"I *press* toward the goal…"

"I *go forward* to the mark…"

In Hot Pursuit

"I *run* toward the goal..."

"I *keep running hard* toward the goal...."

"I *run straight* toward...."

"I keep pursuing the goal..."

"My eyes are fixed on the goal..."

According to Paul in 1 Thessalonians 5:15, what are we to pursue?

What are we to pursue or follow according 1 Timothy 6:11 (spoilers!)?

How about 2 Timothy 2:22 (more spoilers!)?

Considering the verses we have examined, what are some conclusions you can come to regarding the word *pursue* in the New Testament?

Looking at how the word is used in the Old Testament and in the New, what are the similarities you noticed in how this word is used? Record your observations on the Comparison summary.

Are there any differences?

Thinking about the title of this lesson; "What does it mean to pursue," list three or four ideas or points from what you have learned during your study. If you have more, feel free to list them as well. Be sure to include any supporting verses or ideas for each point. You may only have two, but I doubt it.

1.

2.

3.

4.

What insights have you developed from your study of the word pursue?

Fill out the *Outline* summary for this lesson. Use the points you developed for your outline.

Complete the My Take on Things for the this lesson.

Word Summary Date of Study:

Word:	Verse:_____
Strong's Number:	

Definition:

Times Used: ___ **Translated as:**

Other Sources	Definition(s)

Other Bible References	How Used

Putting it My Own Words

Takeaway

Event Summary

Date of Study:

Passage:	Title:	
Time:	Location:	Support
Details		
Details from Other Passages		
Details from Other Sources		
Spiritual or Practical Principles		
Take away		

Word Summary   Date of Study:

Word:	Verse:_____
Strong's Number:	

Definition:

Times Used: ___ Translated as:

Other Sources	Definition(s)

Other Bible References	How Used

Putting it My Own Words

Takeaway

Didactical Summary   Date of Study:

Passage:		Title		
Author:		Thesis:		
Audience:				
Verse	Argument	Statement		Support

Insight

Takeaway

Comparison Summary

VS.

	Scripture	

Insight:

Takeway:

Lesson Outline Summary   Date of Study:

Word:	Title:	
Scripture:	Theme (Context)o:	
Key Words and phrases		

Verse	Points	Support

Takeaway

My Take on Things

My impression
As a result of my study, I discovered and learned something I didn't before
And
And
And
And some more

As a result of my study, I need to work on the following things in my life

I think God wants me to concentrate on:

What is at least one goal I can work toward?

What are the steps I need to take in order to reach my goal?

What kind of timeframe to I wish to accomplish this goal in?

What is the timeframe of the individual steps?

My accountability partner in reaching this goal is

My prayer is

Additional thoughts

Date

Additional Notes:

Let us know, let us pursue the knowledge of the Lord. His going forth is established as the morning; He will come to us like the rain, like the latter and former rain to the earth.

Hosea 6:3

Lesson 2

Pursuing Knowledge

I took a course called the Adult Learner. We looked at the characteristics of adults pursuing educational goals and their motivations. During the course our class completed an assignment which was a learning inventory. It gives you an idea of your preferred style of learning something new. For some, they want to jump in and get their hands dirty; for others they like to gather as much information as possible before even attempting to draw any conclusions or applications.

I am one who likes to gather lots of information. Sometimes, I gather too much for my own good and for those of my prospective students. I want to know everything I can about something, so I tend to think my students do too. Thankfully by the end of my course, by class outlines and presentations were much more streamlined and not so much mind numbing.

When I developed the outline for the study, naturally I felt pursuing knowledge was key. While the other pursuits we will be studying are also important I think they build upon our growing knowledge of God.

The word for knowledge is used 980 times in the Old Testament and 29 times in the new. That brings us up to over 1,000 verses to explore. Add synonyms such as understand, wisdom and a few other and you will get totally confused, lost and discouraged. So you can breathe a sigh of relief – we will not be looking up all those verses – only 500 or so...

Gotcha!

Kidding aside, we will be examining two main passages in this study. Hosea 6 and Proverbs 2:1-10.

In Hot Pursuit

Keep in mind there are three different Old Testament words which are translated into the word knowledge: H998, H1847, and H3045. It is important to consider the connotations and nuances of these words in the context of the passages we will be looking at.

Other words to consider include:

Wisdom – H2451 and H8454

Understand – H995

Understanding – H8394

Discretion – H4209

Hosea 5:15-6:6

Although we are only examining one part of this book, I recommend you read it through to get the big picture.

Hosea is one of those books that at first makes you wonder what God is doing. God instructs the prophet to take a wife of ill-repute. She is unfaithful to Hosea, eventually leaves him and winds up being sold into slavery. In spite of Gomer's behavior Hosea is instructed to love his wife and even purchases her out of slavery.

What we discover is Hosea's relationship with Gomer is a picture of God's relationship with Israel. In spite of the nation's behavior and rebellion, God is still a God of mercy, forgiveness and restoration. As we examine this passage, keep in mind the question of how important is it to pursue the knowledge of God.

Complete the Word Summaries for two of the words translated knowledge:

H1847

H3045

Read Hosea 5:15-6:6. Although this is the main passage we will be examining here, keep in mind the context of the passage.

Complete an Event Summary to get an idea of what has happened for God to indicate that He is returning to His place.

Who is Ephraim?

There are references to Ephraim, Judah and Israel. What is the distinction between them?

Using the Geography summary create a map showing the locations of Ephraim, Israel and Judah.

What does God indicate the reason he is returning to His place?

What do you think His place is?

How long is He going to stay there?

Who does God blame for the way the nation is going?

What is the invitation given in 6:1?

What does the nation recognize in this passage?

What does God promise to do?

What is God love described like in this passage?

In Hot Pursuit

What are the people described as?

When we repent and turn back toward God what happens?

According to this passage knowing God is conditional on what events?

What should we continue doing?

What does God desire more from us that sacrifices?

How does God describe Ephraim in this passage?

How does this compare with how God is described?

The word knowledge appears 3 more times in Hosea. What are the passages?

Complete Verse studies for each passage.

What did you learn during the course of studying this passage?

Based upon these verses why is it important to pursue the knowledge of God?

Proverbs 2:1-11

It almost seems a shame to limit the bulk of our study in Proverbs to these 11 verses. We could look at the entire chapter in relation to our study on pursuing the knowledge of God. Feel free to extend your personal study, but we are limited by time and space.

Proverbs is an interesting book. The bulk of it consists of words of wisdom from a father to his son. There are many verses in this book which comment on the advantages of being wise. This particular passage gives us insight to why we should pursue knowledge of God.

Complete the Didactical summary for this section. This summary is designed for you to focus on the argument that is being presented to the reader.

Write down the logical train of thought the author follows. What must occur before the next step can be taken?

Complete the Word summaries on the synonyms used here as they relate to knowledge. The list has been provided earlier.

Describe the relationships between these words and the knowledge of God as described in Proverbs 2?

Wisdom – H2451

In Hot Pursuit

Wisdom - H8454

Understand – H995

Understanding – H8394

Discretion – H4209

What is the metaphor used here to describe some seeking the knowledge of God?

Why do you think this particular metaphor is used?

If you read the remaining verse in chapter two, (Of course you are going to read them!) What else does acquiring the knowledge of God do for you?

What other Scriptures can you think of speak of the knowledge of God?

How do they shed light on our topic?

What have you learned from your study?

Based on your study complete the Lesson Outline.

What are some practical ways to pursue the knowledge of God?

What steps will you take to pursue your knowledge of God?

Complete the My Take on Things Summary for this lesson.

Word Summary   Date of Study:

Word:	Verse:_____
Strong's Number:	

Definition:

Times Used: ___ Translated as:

Other Sources	Definition(s)

Other Bible References	How Used

Putting it My Own Words

Takeaway

Word Summary

Date of Study:

Word:	Verse:_____
Strong's Number:	

Definition:

Times Used: ___ Translated as:

Other Sources	Definition(s)

Other Bible References	How Used

Putting it My Own Words

Takeaway

Event Summary

Date of Study:

Passage:	Title:	
Time:	Location:	Support
Details		
Details from Other Passages		
Details from Other Sources		
Spiritual or Practical Principles		
Take away		

Event Summary

Date of Study:

Passage:	Title:	
Time:	Location:	**Support**
Details		
Details from Other Passages		
Details from Other Sources		
Spiritual or Practical Principles		
Take away		

Verse Summary

Date of Study:

Title:	
Verse:	
Strong's Number and Definition(s)	**Used Elsewhere**
Quotation? Yes No	**Summary of Original Passage**
Summary of Verse in Context	
Putting it in My Own Words	
Takeaway	

Verse Summary

Date of Study:

Title:	
Verse:	
Strong's Number and Definition(s)	**Used Elsewhere**
Quotation? Yes No	**Summary of Original Passage**

Summary of Verse in Context

Putting it in My Own Words

Takeaway

Verse Summary

Date of Study:

Title:	
Verse:	
Strong's Number and Definition(s)	**Used Elsewhere**
Quotation? Yes No	**Summary of Original Passage**
Summary of Verse in Context	
Putting it in My Own Words	
Takeaway	

Didactical Summary   Date of Study:

Passage:		Title	
Author:		Thesis:	
Audience:			
Verse	**Argument**	**Statement**	**Support**
Insight			
Takeaway			

Word Summary Date of Study:

Word:	Verse:_____
Strong's Number:	

Definition:

Times Used: ___ Translated as:

Other Sources	Definition(s)

Other Bible References	How Used

Putting it My Own Words

Takeaway

Word Summary Date of Study:

Word:	Verse:_____
Strong's Number:	

Definition:

Times Used: ___ Translated as:

Other Sources	Definition(s)

Other Bible References	How Used

Putting it My Own Words

Takeaway

Word Summary Date of Study:

Word:	Verse:_____
Strong's Number:	

Definition:

Times Used: ___ Translated as:

Other Sources	Definition(s)

Other Bible References	How Used

Putting it My Own Words

Takeaway

Word Summary   Date of Study:

Word:	Verse:_____
Strong's Number:	

Definition:

Times Used: ___ Translated as:

Other Sources	Definition(s)

Other Bible References	How Used

Putting it My Own Words

Takeaway

Word Summary   Date of Study:

Word:	Verse:_____
Strong's Number:	

Definition:

Times Used: ___ Translated as:

Other Sources	Definition(s)

Other Bible References	How Used

Putting it My Own Words

Takeaway

Lesson Outline Summary   Date of Study:

Word:	Title:	
Scripture:	Theme (Context)o:	
Key Words and phrases		
Verse	Points	Support
Takeaway		

My Take on Things

My impression
As a result of my study, I discovered and learned something I didn't before
And
And
And
And some more

As a result of my study, I need to work on the following things in my life

I think God wants me to concentrate on:

What is at least one goal I can work toward?

What are the steps I need to take in order to reach my goal?

What kind of timeframe to I wish to accomplish this goal in?

What is the timeframe of the individual steps?

My accountability partner in reaching this goal is

My prayer is

Additional thoughts

Date

Additional Notes:

In Hot Pursuit

Twelve Things God Wants Us to Pursue

Seek Peace and pursue it.

Psalm 34:14b

Lesson Three

Pursuing Peace

In this study we will be looking at a topic which most of us crave to have: Peace. But what do we define as peace. Is it a cessation of war, a special place where we go to get away from the hustle and bustle of our busy lives or something else entirely?

There is a peace we should be actively chasing after, it is God's peace. The Bible tells us five times to pursue peace. But what kind of peace it that? Let's start our study by taking a look at Psalm 34. As we consider the words of this Psalm keep in mind the historical context of why this Psalm was written.

We should also consider that of the twelve things God wants us to pursue, we are instructed to pursue peace more than all the other topics we will be studying. In my books it means peace very important to God. If it is important to God it should also be important to us.

If you are unfamiliar with studying Biblical poetry I have included an excerpt *from The Bible School Dropout's Guide to More Bible Study.* It would be a really nice gesture and a vote of confidence if you were to purchase a copy of my book. (This is my shameless marketing tact for this book!).

Complete the Word Summaries for the Old and New Testament Words for Peace.

H7965

Page | 51

In Hot Pursuit

G1515

Psalm 34:8-14

Psalm 34 is a beautiful Psalm. Well... they are all pretty good. You should read them sometime. We could spend the entire lesson just studying Psalm 34. However, since this is only a piece of the puzzle we will only be focusing on part of it. I do encourage you to spend some more time on this and other Psalms in the future.

To save some time I am including some information which I would normally let you discover on your own. However, I expect you to fill in the pieces.

The introduction to the Psalm indicates it was written after David pretended to be insane to escape an enemy, King Abimelech of Gath. This was not a good time in David's life. He was on the run hunted by Saul.

Saul had attempted to kill him and was actively searching for the person God had chosen to replace him. During this time of fearing for his life, David wrote about what he learned. If you turn to 1 Samuel 21 you can read all about it. If you go back a chapter or two or three (as well as forward) you will get a bigger picture.

It is ironic the "fool" or "insane person" wrote this poem of wisdom and praise.

The poem is written as an acrostic. Each verse except one starts with a letter from the Hebrew alphabet. We don't know that because we are not reading it in the original language. The missing letter (*waw* - ו) would have been about where verse five is.

In case you've done your homework, the next questions you ask should be: I thought the Hebrew alphabet was 22 letters? So if one letter was dropped out, how come I am looking at 22 verses?

The answer: Verse 22 is a summary of the Psalm and not a part of the acrostic pattern.

Psalm 34 is normally divided into four sections: 1-3, 4-7, 8-14 and 15-22. I am not going to go into more detail than this with the exception of 8-14. This is the instructional part of the Psalm. It will be up to you to fill in the details on the rest of the Psalm.

I have included a *Chapter Summary* for you in case you want to pursue this Psalm more. I strongly suggest you do. It will help in your analysis.

Let's focus on verses 11 – 14.

What does the writer infer in how he addresses his audience?

What does he want to teach them?

Complete the *Word* summaries for the following words:

Fear – H3374

Depart – H5493

Keep – H5341

Seek – H1245

What does the writer means when he says he will teach them the fear of the Lord?

What are the commands he issues as a part of showing our reverence for God?

What does the author imply in verse 14?

In Hot Pursuit

Look at the verses which precede this section. How does this show what David has learned from his experiences?

Romans 14:19

Ok, technically this verse doesn't specifically instruct us to pursue peace. It instructs us to seek, follow after or pursue (depending on the translation you are using) the things which make for peace.

So what does this mean? Paul said there are things which produce peace. What are they? Luckily we have a clue to follow: The word "therefore."

Why is this a good thing? Well, when we see this word we can assume that we are reading the conclusion to Paul's argument. So by looking at the verse in context, we should be able to figure out what are those things we are to pursue in order to get to the goal of peace.

Read verses 14-23 to get an idea of the argument Paul is creating. You can probably read the entire chapter, if you think you have the time, but that is not totally necessary; just highly recommended.

Complete the *Didactic Summary* to discover Paul's argument. (Didactic is a fancy word for teaching)

What are the things Paul is talking about?

What is the kingdom of God according to this passage?

What does walking in love mean?

Complete the *Comparison Summary* between Psalm 34 and Roman 14.

Are there any similarities?

Are there any differences?

2 Timothy 2:22

Complete the *Verse Summary*.

What insight from this verse and its context verses add to what you have already learned from the other passages?

Are there any common threads between these three passages?

What are they?

Hebrews 12:4

Complete the Verse Summary.

In Hot Pursuit

Have this verse and the surrounding verses add anything to what has already been discovered by your investigation?

What is or are they?

According to this verse what is the significance to pursuing peace?

1 Peter 3:11

Complete the Verse Summary.

What did you learn from the words in this verse?

And one more time: Have this verse and the surrounding verses add anything to what has already been discovered by your investigation?.

Why do you think the difference is between seeking and pursuing peace?

What verse or passage tells us how or why we have peace with God? Hint: It hasn't been discussed in the list of passages we have examined... but it can be found somewhere in Romans.... Five... I think.

Putting it All Together

Looking over the information you have gathered complete the Similarities and Differences Summary and then answer the following questions. You do not have to use all the spaces provided on the summary. If you find more information you can use the Additional Notes page.

When we look at the five passages together what are we to avoid in our pursuit?

What are we to do in our pursuit of peace?

Why is it important to pursue peace?

How would you summarize the pursuit of peace?

Complete the *Lesson Outline*.

In Hot Pursuit

What have you learned about pursuing peace?

Complete *My Take on Things*.

Word Summary Date of Study:

Word:	Verse:_____
Strong's Number:	

Definition:

Times Used: ___ Translated as:

Other Sources	Definition(s)

Other Bible References	How Used

Putting it My Own Words

Takeaway

Word Summary Date of Study:

Word:	Verse:_____
Strong's Number:	
Definition:	
Times Used: ___ Translated as:	

Other Sources	Definition(s)

Other Bible References	How Used

Putting it My Own Words

Takeaway

Poetry Summary

Date of Study:

Passage: Psalm 34:11-14	Title:

Historical Context: 1 Samuel 21: 10-15

Verse:	Images:	Support

Insight from the Context:

Insight from Other Scripture or Sources	Source

Takeaway:

Chapter Summary

Date of Study:

Book:	Title:	
Passage:	Theme (Context):	
Key Words:	Key Verse:	

Verse	Points	Support

Take Away

Word Summary   Date of Study:

Word:	Verse:_____
Strong's Number:	

Definition:

Times Used: ___ Translated as:

Other Sources	Definition(s)

Other Bible References	How Used

Putting it My Own Words

Takeaway

Word Summary Date of Study:

Word:	Verse:_____
Strong's Number:	

Definition:

Times Used: ___ Translated as:

Other Sources	Definition(s)

Other Bible References	How Used

Putting it My Own Words

Takeaway

Word Summary Date of Study:

Word:	Verse:_____
Strong's Number:	

Definition:

Times Used: ___ Translated as:

Other Sources	Definition(s)

Other Bible References	How Used

Putting it My Own Words

Takeaway

Word Summary   Date of Study:

Word:	Verse:_____
Strong's Number:	

Definition:

Times Used: ___ Translated as:

Other Sources	Definition(s)

Other Bible References	How Used

Putting it My Own Words

Takeaway

Didactical Summary   Date of Study:

Passage:		Title		
Author:		Thesis:		
Audience:				
Verse	Argument	Statement		Support
Insight				
Takeaway				

Comparison Summary

VS.

	Scripture	

Insight:

Takeaway:

Verse Summary

Date of Study:

Title:	
Verse:	
Strong's Number and Definition(s)	**Used Elsewhere**
Quotation? Yes No	**Summary of Original Passage**
Summary of Verse in Context	
Putting it in My Own Words	
Takeaway	

Verse Summary

Date of Study:

Title:	
Verse:	
Strong's Number and Definition(s)	**Used Elsewhere**
Quotation? Yes No	**Summary of Original Passage**
Summary of Verse in Context	
Putting it in My Own Words	
Takeaway	

Verse Summary

Date of Study:

Title:	
Verse:	
Strong's Number and Definition(s)	**Used Elsewhere**
Quotation? Yes No	**Summary of Original Passage**
Summary of Verse in Context	
Putting it in My Own Words	
Takeaway	

Similarities and Differences

Similarity or Difference	Psalm 34	Romans 14	2 Timothy 2	Hebrews 12	1 Peter 3

Lesson Outline Summary

Date of Study:

Word:	Title:	
Scripture:	Theme (Context)o:	
Key Words and phrases		
Verse	Points	Support
Takeaway		

My Take on Things

My impression
As a result of my study, I discovered and learned something I didn't before
And
And
And
And some more

As a result of my study, I need to work on the following things in my life
I think God wants me to concentrate on:
What is at least one goal I can work toward?
What are the steps I need to take in order to reach my goal?
What kind of timeframe to I wish to accomplish this goal in?

What is the timeframe of the individual steps?

My accountability partner in reaching this goal is

My prayer is

Additional thoughts

Date

Additional Notes:

Pursue peace with all people, and holiness, without which no one will see the Lord:

Hebrew 12:14

Lesson Four

Pursuing Holiness

Holiness is one of those things which are difficult to get a handle on. We won't have the time and space to do an in-depth study of this important topic. Many people have written books about what holiness is and how to get it. Some of them are very good and some of them are a bunch of hooey.

If you wish to examine this topic further, I recommend Jerry Bridges book *The Pursuit of Holiness*.

Although there is only one verse which commands us to pursue holiness, there are many verses which make being holy a command and a part of our spiritual walk. Don't worry. We won't be examining every verse…. Only half or so…

Ok. Let's get started by putting together a working definition of holiness.

Complete the *Word Summaries* for holiness in the Old and New Testaments. I have included a reference chart for your convenience.

H6944

G38

G41

G42

G2150

G2412

G3742

In order to help speed things along a bit I've included a list of the reference where these words are used. If you are using a Bible other than the King James you will probably see different words used than the ones listed.

You will notice that especially for the Old Testament, it is translated several ways, most notably as the word "holy." Like with some of our other word studies you don't have to examine every passage, but only enough to get an idea of how the word is defined and used in the context of the passages you have examined.

In a Nutshell

What have you learned based upon your study of the Old Testament word? You can use a much or little detail as you like. Remember we are not doing an exhaustive study, just attempting to get a handle on our subject.

Cite the passage you are referring to with the statements you make.

Now it is time to look how the words are used in the New Testament. The same rules apply for your conclusions about how holiness is defined in the Old Testament.

Based upon your brief study of the word "holiness" what is your working definition?

Hebrews 12

I like reading the book of Hebrews. It has one main theme: Jesus Christ is the BEST!!!! The author's only goal was to present to his audience that Jesus was the better prophet, king, priest, son, sacrifice, etc. It is a great book to read and study.

Now that being said, some of the most head scratching passages ever written in the Bible occur in this book. I am not saying that to frighten you away. You should also breathe a sigh of relief that the passage we will be looking at is not the most hair pulling of them... you will only lose a few strands.

This passage starts with "therefore." And what does that mean? Come on. You should know this. We touched on it in the last lesson. At least I think it was the last lesson.

Usually the word indicates he is concluding an argument. This means you might want to take a look at some of the verses before this passage to see what he was talking about. It may have a bearing on your conclusions for this passage.

Complete the *Verse Summaries* for verses 12-17.

What did the author write about before the "therefore" in verse 12?

What are the commands he issues in Verses 12-15?

1.

2.

3.

4.

5.

What are the dangers we are to look out for?

1.

2.

3.

What do you think falling short of God's grace means? (I'll tell you right now it doesn't mean you lose your salvation... but that is for another study and another book.)

How about a root of bitterness? What is it and how would it affect your pursuit of holiness?

Why do you think Esau is cited as an example of a fornicator or profane person?

The author starts this section with a quote from Isaiah 35:3. What was that passage about and how do you think it could relate to what he was saying to his audience?

How does Matthew 5:8 shed light on this passage we are looking at?

Would people who seek peace and holiness be considered pure of heart?

Explain your answer and use Scripture references to support your argument.

Why is it important to pursue holiness?

What other verses support the idea of pursuing holiness? Here you would have to look for similar concepts, as we already know this is the only place we are commanded to pursue holiness.

Write down the references and the reasons they would support the concept of pursuing holiness. Please use at least four examples.

1.

2.

In Hot Pursuit

3.

4.

How would you summarize the pursuit of holiness?

Complete the *Lesson Outline*.

What have you learned about pursuing holiness?

Complete *My Take on Things*.

P a g e | **84**

Word Summary   Date of Study:

Word:	Verse:_____
Strong's Number:	

Definition:

Times Used: ___ Translated as:

Other Sources	Definition(s)

Other Bible References	How Used

Putting it My Own Words

Takeaway

Word Summary   Date of Study:

Word:	Verse:_____
Strong's Number:	

Definition:

Times Used: ___ Translated as:

Other Sources	Definition(s)

Other Bible References	How Used

Putting it My Own Words

Takeaway

Word Summary Date of Study:

Word:	Verse:_____
Strong's Number:	

Definition:

Times Used: ___ Translated as:

Other Sources	Definition(s)

Other Bible References	How Used

Putting it My Own Words

Takeaway

Word Summary Date of Study:

Word:	Verse:_____
Strong's Number:	

Definition:

Times Used: ___ Translated as:

Other Sources	Definition(s)

Other Bible References	How Used

Putting it My Own Words

Takeaway

Word Summary   Date of Study:

Word:	Verse:_____
Strong's Number:	

Definition:

Times Used: ___ Translated as:

Other Sources	Definition(s)

Other Bible References	How Used

Putting it My Own Words

Takeaway

Word Summary   Date of Study:

Word:	Verse:_____
Strong's Number:	

Definition:

Times Used: ___ Translated as:

Other Sources	Definition(s)

Other Bible References	How Used

Putting it My Own Words

Takeaway

Word Summary   Date of Study:

Word:	Verse:_____
Strong's Number:	

Definition:

Times Used: ___ Translated as:

Other Sources	Definition(s)

Other Bible References	How Used

Putting it My Own Words

Takeaway

In Hot Pursuit

Verse Summary

Date of Study:

Title:	
Verse:	
Strong's Number and Definition(s)	**Used Elsewhere**
Quotation? Yes No	**Summary of Original Passage**

Summary of Verse in Context

Putting it in My Own Words

Takeaway

Verse Summary

Date of Study:

Title:	
Verse:	
Strong's Number and Definition(s)	**Used Elsewhere**
Quotation? Yes No	**Summary of Original Passage**
Summary of Verse in Context	
Putting it in My Own Words	
Takeaway	

Verse Summary

Date of Study:

Title:	
Verse:	
Strong's Number and Definition(s)	**Used Elsewhere**
Quotation? Yes No	**Summary of Original Passage**

Summary of Verse in Context

Putting it in My Own Words

Takeaway

Verse Summary

Date of Study:

Title:	
Verse:	
Strong's Number and Definition(s)	**Used Elsewhere**
Quotation? Yes No	**Summary of Original Passage**
Summary of Verse in Context	
Putting it in My Own Words	
Takeaway	

Verse Summary

Date of Study:

Title:	
Verse:	
Strong's Number and Definition(s)	**Used Elsewhere**
Quotation? Yes No	**Summary of Original Passage**
Summary of Verse in Context	
Putting it in My Own Words	
Takeaway	

Lesson Outline Summary

Date of Study:

Word:	Title:	
Scripture:	Theme (Context):	
Key Words and phrases		
Verse	Points	Support
Takeaway		

My Take on Things

My impression
As a result of my study, I discovered and learned something I didn't before
And
And
And
And some more

As a result of my study, I need to work on the following things in my life

I think God wants me to concentrate on:

What is at least one goal I can work toward?

What are the steps I need to take in order to reach my goal?

What kind of timeframe to I wish to accomplish this goal in?

What is the timeframe of the individual steps?

My accountability partner in reaching this goal is

My prayer is

Additional thoughts

Date

Additional Notes:

Old Testament usage based on KJV

H6944

קֹדֶשׁ

qoˆdesh

Occurrences: 458

Holy, 303

Exo 3:5,
Exo 12:16 (2),
Exo 15:13,
Exo 16:23,
Exo 22:31,
Exo 26:33-34 (3),
Exo 28:2,
 Exo 28:4,
Exo 28:29,
Exo 28:35,
Exo 28:38 (2),
Exo 28:43,
Exo 29:6,
Exo 29:29-30 (2),
Exo 29:33-34 (2),
Exo 29:37 (2),
Exo 30:10,
Exo 30:25 (2),
Exo 30:29,
Exo 30:31-32 (3),
Exo 30:35-37 (3),
Exo 31:10-11 (2),
Exo 31:14-15 (2),
Exo 35:2,
Exo 35:19 (2),
Exo 35:21,
Exo 37:29,
Exo 38:24,
Exo 39:1 (2),
Exo 39:30,
Exo 39:41 (2),
Exo 40:9-10 (2),
Exo 40:13,
Lev 2:3,
Lev 2:10,

Lev 6:15-17 (3),
Lev 6:25,
Lev 6:29-30 (2),
Lev 7:1,
Lev 7:6,
Lev 10:9-10 (2),
Lev 10:12,
Lev 10:17-18 (4),
Lev 14:13 (2),
Lev 16:2-4 (4),
Lev 16:16-17 (2),
Lev 16:20,
Lev 16:23,
Lev 16:27,
Lev 16:32-33 (2),
Lev 19:24,
Lev 20:3,
Lev 21:6,
Lev 21:22,
Lev 22 (14), (2),
Lev 23:4 (3),
Lev 23:7-8 (2),
Lev 23:20-21 (2),
Lev 23:24,
Lev 23:27,
Lev 23:35-37 (3),
Lev 24:9,
Lev 25:12,
Lev 27:9-10 (2),
Lev 27:14,
Lev 27:21,
Lev 27:23,
Lev 27:28,
Lev 27:30,

Lev 27:32-33 (2),
Num 4:4,
Num 4:15,
Num 4:19-20 (2),
Num 5:9,
Num 6:20,
Num 18:9-10 (4),
Num 18:17,
Num 18:19,
Num 18:32,
Num 28:7,
Num 28:18,
Num 28:25-26 (2), Num 29:1,
Num 29:7,
Num 29:12,
Num 31:6,
Deu 12:25-26 (2),
Jos 5:15 (2),
1Sa 21:5,
1Ki 6:16,
1Ki 7:50,
1Ki 8:4,
1Ki 8:6,
1Ki 8:8,
1Ki 8:10,
1Ch 6:49,
1Ch 16:10,
1Ch 16:35,
1Ch 22:19,
1Ch 23:13,
1Ch 23:28,
1Ch 23:32,
1Ch 29:3,
1Ch 29:16,

2Ch 3:8,
2Ch 3:10,
2Ch 4:22,
2Ch 5:5,
2Ch 5:7,
2Ch 8:11 (2),
2Ch 23:6,
2Ch 29:5,
2Ch 29:7,
2Ch 30:27,
2Ch 31:6,
2Ch 31:14,
2Ch 35:3,
2Ch 35:5,
2Ch 35:13,
Ezr 2:63,
Ezr 8:28 (2),
Ezr 9:2,
Ezr 9:8,
Neh 7:65,
Neh 9:14,
Neh 10:31,
Neh 10:33,
Neh 11:1,
Neh 11:18,
Neh 12:47,
Psa 2:6,
Psa 3:4,
Psa 5:7,
Psa 11:4,
Psa 15:1,
Psa 20:6,
Psa 24:3,
Psa 28:2,
Psa 33:21,

Psa 43:3,
Psa 51:11,
Psa 68:5,
Psa 68:17,
Psa 87:1 (2),
Psa 89:20,
Psa 98:1,
Psa 99:9,
Psa 103:1,
Psa 105:3,
Psa 105:42,
Psa 106:47,
Psa 138:2,
Psa 145:21,
Pro 20:25,
Isa 6:13,
Isa 11:9,
Isa 27:13,
Isa 48:2,
Isa 52:1,
Isa 52:10,
Isa 56:7,
Isa 58:13 (2),
Isa 62:12,
Isa 63:10-11 (2),
Isa 65:10-11 (3),
Isa 65:25,
Isa 66:20,
Jer 11:15,
Jer 25:30,
Jer 31:40,
Jer 50:29,
Eze 20:39-40 (2),
Eze 22:8,
Eze 22:26 (2),

Eze 28:14,
Eze 36:20-22 (3),
Eze 36:38,
Eze 39:7 (2),
Eze 39:25,
Eze 41:4,
Eze 42:13-14 (4),
Eze 43:7-8 (2),
Eze 43:12,
Eze 44:8,
Eze 44:13 (2),
Eze 44:19,
Eze 44:23,
Eze 45:1 (2),
Eze 45:3-4 (2),
Eze 45:6-7 (3),
Eze 46:19,
Eze 48:10,
48:12,
Eze 48:14,
Eze 48:18 (2),
Eze 48:20-21 (3),
Dan 9:16,
Dan 9:20,
Dan 9:24 (2),
Dan 11:28,
Dan 11:30 (2),
Dan 11:45,
Dan 12:7,
Joe 2:1,
Joe 3:17 (2),
Amo 2:7, Oba
1:16,
Jon
2:4,

Jon 2:7,
Mic 1:2,
Hab 2:20,
Zec 2:11-13 (4),
Zec 8:3

Sanctuary, 55

Exo 30:13,
Exo 30:24,
Exo 36:1,
Exo 36:3-4 (2),
Exo 36:6,
Exo 38:24-27 (4),
Lev 4:6,
Lev 5:15,
Lev 10:4,
Lev 27:3, Lev
27:25,
Num 3:28,
Num 3:31-32 (2),
Num 3:47,
Num 3:50,
Num 4:12,
Num 4:15-16 (3),
Num 7:9,
Num 7:86,
Num 8:19,
Num 18:3,
Num 18:5,
Num 18:16,
1Ch 9:29,
1Ch 24:5,
2Ch 30:19,
Psa 63:2 (2),
Psa 68:24,
Psa 74:3,
77:13,
Psa 78:54,
Psa 102:19,

Psa 134:2 (2), Psa 150:1,
Isa 43:28,
Lam 4:1,
Eze 41:21,
Eze 41:23,
Eze 42:20,
Eze 44:27 (2),
Eze 45:2,
Dan 8:13-14 (2),
Dan 9:26

,

Zep 3:4

Most, 47

Exo 26:33-34 (2),
Exo 29:37,
Exo 30:10,
Exo 30:29,
Exo 30:36,
Exo 40:10,
Lev 2:3,
Lev 2:10,
Lev 6:17,
Lev 6:25,
Lev 6:29,
Lev 7:1,
Lev 7:6,
Lev 10:12,
Lev 10:17,
Lev 14:13,
Lev 21:22,
Lev 24:9,
Lev 27:28,
Num 4:4,
Num 4:19,
Num 18:9-10 (3),
Num 24:16,
Deu 32:8,
2Sa 22:14,
1Ki 6:16,
1Ki 7:50,
1Ki 8:6,
1Ch 6:49,
1Ch 23:13,
2Ch 3:8,
2Ch 3:10,
2Ch 4:22,
2Ch 5:7,
2Ch 31:14,

Neh 7:65,
Eze 41:4,
Eze 42:13 (2),
Eze 44:12-13 (2),
Eze 45:3,
Eze 48:12,
Dan 9:24

holiness, 30

Exo 15:11,
Exo 28:36,
Exo 39:30,
1Ch 16:29,
2Ch 20:21,
2Ch 31:18, Psa
29:2,
Psa 30:4,
Psa 47:8,
Psa 48:1,
Psa 60:6,
Psa 89:35,
Psa 93:5,
Psa 96:9,
Psa 97:12,
Psa 108:7,
Psa 110:3,
Isa 23:18,
Isa 62:8-9 (2),
Isa 63:15,
Isa 63:18,
Jer 2:3,
Jer 23:9,
Jer 31:23,
Amo 4:2,
Oba 1:17,
Zec 14:20-21 (2),
Mal 2:11

dedicated, 12

1Ki 7:51,

1Ki 15:15 (2),

2Ki 12:4,

1Ch 26:20,

1Ch 26:26,

1Ch 28:12,

2Ch 5:1,

2Ch 15:18 (2),

2Ch 24:7,

2Ch 31:12

hallowed, 9

Lev 12:4,

Lev 19:8,

Num 5:10,

Num 18:8,

Deu 26:13,

1Sa 21:4,

1Sa 21:6,

2Ki 12:18 (2)

consecrated, 1

Jos 6:18-19 (2)

saints, 1

Deu 33:2

New Testament
uses based upon
KJV
G38

ἁγιασμός

hagiasmos

Occurrences: 10

Holiness, 5

Rom 6:19,
Rom 6:22,
1Th 4:7,
1Ti 2:15,
Heb 12:14

Sanctification, 5

1Co 1:30,
1Th 4:3-4 (2),
2Th 2:13,
1Pe 1:2

G41
ἁγιότης
hagiotēs
Occurrences: 1
Holiness, 1

Heb 12:10 (2)

G42
ἁγιωσύνη
hagiōsunē
Occurrences: 3
Holiness, 3

Rom 1:4,
2Co 7:1,
1Th 3:13

G2412

ἱεροπρεπής

hieroprepēs

Occurrences: 2

Becometh, 1

Tit 2:3

Holiness, 1
Tit 2:3 (2)

G2150

εὐσέβεια

eusebeia

Occurrences: 15

Godliness, 14

1Ti 2:2,
1Ti 3:16,
1Ti 4:7-8 (2),
1Ti 6:3,
1Ti 6:5-6 (2),
1Ti 6:11,
2Ti 3:5,
Tit 1:1,
2Pe 1:3,
2Pe 1:6-7 (2),
2Pe 3:11

Holiness, 1

Act 3:11-12 (2)

G3742

ὁσιότης

hosiotēs

Occurrences: 2

holiness, 2

Luk 1:75,
Eph 4:24

In Hot Pursuit

But you, O man of God, flee these things and pursue righteousness, godliness, faith, love, patience, gentleness.

1 Timothy 6:11

Lesson Five

Pursuing Righteousness

If I were putting subtitles under my chapter headings instead of starting the lesson quoting a passage, I would have written "Pursuing the Standard" under the word "Righteousness."

For one thing, I would have to redesign the look of all my lessons even though this is the fifth one. It means we are almost at the halfway mark of our study. When you complete the next lesson then you will be halfway through. Give yourself a high-five at how far you've come!

The second reason is this: Spoilers. If I had used the phrase "Pursuing the Standard" as a subheading for the chapter I would have given you an all important clue to how to approach this particular study. I am for encouraging you to study the Scriptures for yourself with nothing from me which will prejudice your conclusions.

So I won't be using the phrase "Pursuing the Standard" as a subheading for this particular lesson.

Like some of the other topics we have been exploring and will explore, the Bible has a lot to say about righteousness. The word is used over 200 times in the Old Testament and almost 100 in the new. We will be concentrating on what the New Testament has to say a about this topic as all the references about pursuing righteous are New Testament Ones.

If you want to expand your understanding of righteousness I encourage you to dive into a detailed a study as you want to. I'll be honest with you. I would have liked to have packed everything I could find about this fascinating topic. But we are not looking at the entire scope of righteousness, only the pursuit of it.

In Hot Pursuit

One of the things about this topic and other is it is a very abstract concept. There are many theories and ideas floating out there, some which are sound and some which are so far based outside the realm of reality you have to dial a different area code to connect.

So we want to keep it real and keep it brief. I started looking at the references myself when I was preparing this study and the more I examined the more I wanted to study it more. But that's just me. I had to remind myself this study is a TOPICAL study on PURSUING righteousness, not a study on the topic or doctrine of righteousness. However, that may be an idea for a future study... mmmmm.

Ok let's get a definition of righteousness we can use as our "standard."

Complete the *Word Summary* for G1343.

As part of your study, look at the specific verses where the phrase is. Romans 9:30-32, 1 Timothy 6:11 and 2 Timothy 2:22. Complete *Phrase Summaries* for these passages.

Here is a list of references you can use as you work to produce a definition of righteousness. You don't have to use them, but they are pretty good in giving us a basic idea.

Isaiah 64:6, Matthew 6:33, Romans 1:17, 3:23-26, 4:3-22, 5:17-21; 6:12-20; 10:3-10; 14:7; Galatians 3:21; Philippians 3:9; Titus 3:5; James 1:20. Don't forget to consider your verses in the light of the context of where they are and considering our specific topic of pursuing righteousness.

What is your working "stand... er... definition of righteousness?

Complete the *Didactic Summary* for Romans 9:30-32. Take note of the opening question, "What shall we say then?" It sounds like he is concluding an argument which he was presenting before. I recommend you take a look at the preceding section to get an idea of what the argument is about.

Based on your study so far, what is the law of righteousness?

Why was Israel unsuccessful in attaining the law of righteousness?

According to this passage, what is the main factor in successfully pursuing righteousness?

Complete the *Verse Summary* for 1 Timothy 6:11.

What are "these things?"

Why do people pursue these things?

What are we to pursue instead?

What do they have in common?

If you were to read the next few verses, what other things are we commanded to do?

In Hot Pursuit
How do these commands fit with what we are commanded to pursue?

Complete the *Verse Summary* for 2 Timothy 2:22.

How is this list of pursuits different from the instructions given to Timothy in the first letter?

Pull back and look at verses 19 – 26. Complete the *Didactical Summary* for this section.

What is the argument Paul is using for Timothy in order to urge him to pursue righteousness?

Expanding our context of this passage by a few more verses, what are some of the other commands we are given which help our quest for righteousness?

What can we understand about God's standards when we read these passages?

Why is it important to strive to conform to God's standards?

How would you summarize the pursuit of righteousness?

Complete the *Lesson Outline*.

What have you learned about pursuing righteousness?

Complete *My Take on Things*.

Word Summary   Date of Study:

Word:	Verse:_____
Strong's Number:	

Definition:

Times Used: ___ Translated as:

Other Sources	Definition(s)

Other Bible References	How Used

Putting it My Own Words

Takeaway

Phrase Summary

Date of Study

Verse: Romans 9:30		Phrase: Righteousness of Faith	
Strong's #	**Definitions:**	**Other Sources**	**Definitions**
Other verses:	**Meaning in Context:**		**Support:**
Literal meaning:		**Figurative or idiomatic meaning:**	
What insight does this give me?			

Phrase Summary

Date of Study

Verse: Romans 9:31		Phrase: Righteousness of Law	
Strong's #	**Definitions:**	**Other Sources**	**Definitions**
Other verses:	**Meaning in Context:**		**Support:**
Literal meaning:		**Figurative or idiomatic meaning:**	
What insight does this give me?			

Phrase Summary

Date of Study

Verse: 1 Timothy 6:11		Phrase: Pursue righteousness	
Strong's #	**Definitions:**	**Other Sources**	**Definitions**
Other verses:	**Meaning in Context:**		**Support:**
Literal meaning:		**Figurative or idiomatic meaning:**	
What insight does this give me?			

Phrase Summary   Date of Study

Verse: 2 Timothy 2:22		Phrase: Pursue righteousness	
Strong's #	**Definitions:**	**Other Sources**	**Definitions**
Other verses:	**Meaning in Context:**		**Support:**
Literal meaning:		**Figurative or idiomatic meaning:**	
What insight does this give me?			

Didactical Summary   Date of Study:

Passage:		Title	
Author:		Thesis:	
Audience:			
Verse	Argument	Statement	Support
Insight			
Takeaway			

Verse Summary Date of Study:

Title:	
Verse:	
Strong's Number and Definition(s)	**Used Elsewhere**
Quotation? Yes No	**Summary of Original Passage**
Summary of Verse in Context	
Putting it in My Own Words	
Takeaway	

Verse Summary

Date of Study:

Title:	
Verse:	
Strong's Number and Definition(s)	**Used Elsewhere**
Quotation? Yes No	**Summary of Original Passage**
Summary of Verse in Context	
Putting it in My Own Words	
Takeaway	

Didactical Summary   Date of Study:

Passage:		Title	
Author:		Thesis:	
Audience:			

Verse	Argument	Statement	Support

Insight

Takeaway

Lesson Outline Summary

Date of Study:

Word:	Title:	
Scripture:	Theme (Context):	

Key Words and phrases

Verse	Points	Support

Takeaway

My Take on Things

My impression

As a result of my study, I discovered and learned something I didn't before

And

And

And

And some more

As a result of my study, I need to work on the following things in my life

I think God wants me to concentrate on:
What is at least one goal I can work toward?
What are the steps I need to take in order to reach my goal?
What kind of timeframe to I wish to accomplish this goal in?
What is the timeframe of the individual steps?

My accountability partner in reaching this goal is

My prayer is

Additional thoughts

Date

Additional Notes:

Follow after... faith

1 Timothy 6:11

Lesson Six

Pursuing Faith

Faith is a central theme of the Bible and it is no surprise it is a thing God wants us to pursue.

We discovered in our last lesson that the correct righteousness we pursue is that which is of faith. Depending on our own standards doesn't earn God's approval or favor. It is the righteousness we receive through Jesus Christ by faith.

I found it interesting both of the references we are looking at were directed toward the same man. Paul instructed Timothy to pursue faith in both of his letters. So let's take a look at faith and find out why and how we should pursue it.

By now you know the exercise. We start our study by developing a working definition of faith. I could just quote Hebrews 11:1 but what would the fun be in that? Besides, some of your work has already been done in previous lessons. That is one of the hallmarks of learning; build on what you have done before. Cool, eh?

Complete the Word Summary for the word faith – G4102.

What did you discover in your exploration of this word?

Complete the Verse Summary for Hebrews 11:1

According to Hebrews 11 in general, what does or did faith do?

List some of the passages which indicate to us the important of faith in our spiritual journey. Besides each reference explain why you chose them.

Now write down your working definition of faith.

With this definition in mind take a look at 1 Timothy 6.

Verse 11 starts with the word "but." This means Paul is drawing a comparison or a contrast to something. What is he drawing a comparison of?

Note your findings on the comparison chart.

What are your conclusions on this comparison?

Starting with 2 Timothy 2:15 complete the *Didactical Summary*.

What is the main point of Paul's argument?

List the instructions Paul has given Timothy in this passage?

Based upon your study why would Paul give the instruction to pursue faith?

How would you summarize the pursuit of faith?

Complete the *Lesson Outline*.

What have you learned about pursuing faith?

Complete *My Take on Things*.

Word Summary Date of Study:

Word:	Verse:_____
Strong's Number:	
Definition:	
Times Used: ___ Translated as:	

Other Sources	Definition(s)

Other Bible References	How Used

Putting it My Own Words	

Takeaway

Comparison Summary

VS.

	Scripture	

Insight:

Takeaway:

Didactical Summary   Date of Study:

Passage:		Title		
Author:		Thesis:		
Audience:				
Verse	**Argument**	**Statement**		**Support**
Insight				
Takeaway				

Lesson Outline Summary

Date of Study:

Word:	Title:	
Scripture:	Theme (Context):	
Key Words and phrases		
Verse	Points	Support
Takeaway		

My Take on Things

My impression
As a result of my study, I discovered and learned something I didn't before
And
And
And
And some more
As a result of my study, I need to work on the following things in my life

I think God wants me to concentrate on:
What is at least one goal I can work toward?
What are the steps I need to take in order to reach my goal?
What kind of timeframe to I wish to accomplish this goal in?
What is the timeframe of the individual steps?

My accountability partner in reaching this goal is

My prayer is

Additional thoughts

Date

Additional Notes:

Pursue love, and desire spiritual gifts...

1 Corinthians 14:1a

Lesson Seven

Pursuing Love

Mentioned 116 times in the New Testament alone, love is an important topic. And why should it not be? Love is a sought after commodity. Most people have ideas of love which consist of flowers and candy and good feelings. But love goes far beyond that.

Three times we are encouraged to pursue love. We have already looked at couple of those passages already, so you should be familiar with them. The third is part of a conclusion to an argument Paul made in probably one of the most recognizable passages we know: 1 Corinthians 13.

This topic, like most of those in this book, has been explored, studied, examined and written about in great detail. We have so many ideas about what love is and what we do or don't do to get it or give it or pass it along. So it may or may not come as a surprise to you that we are commanded to pursue it.

So let's take a look at how the Bible defines this type of love and its characteristics which we should so eagerly desire to seek after and claim for ourselves.

It should also come as no surprise to you then that we are starting at pretty much the same place for this study as the other lessons: definitions. Well, only one... for now...

Complete the Word Summary for G26

What did you discover about this word?

In Hot Pursuit

What is your working definition?

Review your notes on 1 Timothy 6:11 in lesson five and six. It's kinda nice having some of the work already done.

Why would the pursuit of love be included in 1 Timothy 6:11 as a goal in fleeing the things mentioned in the previous verses?

Review your notes on 2 Timothy 2:22 from lessons 3, 5 and six.

Why do you think Paul would include the pursuit of love in this passage of Scripture?

Paul told Timothy twice to pursue love. Why do you think he did this?

In order to get an idea of the big picture read 1 Corinthians 13-14.

Fill out the Love Is Summary.

What is Paul's summary in his definition of love?

Starting in 1 Corinthians 14, Paul continues his argument of the superiority of love over spiritual gifts. It should be noted the word "gifts" doesn't appear in the original language. The word was supplied by the translators to help clarify what Paul was talking about. You could use the word "things" instead of "gifts."

Keep in mind there were many issues and problems with the church in Corinth and Paul was attempting to address them. The Corinthian Christians had gotten their priorities out of whack and Paul was attempting to straighten them out.

Remember this study is examining the things God want us to pursue. That is our focus, not on which thing is more important, but what and why we are told to pursue love.

Complete the Didactive Summary for verses 1 – 12.

Do a word study on the word "prophecy." – G4395

What do you think the word means?

Based on your word study, what are some other definitions of this word?

What is significant about prophecy in this passage?

What is the basis of Paul's argument for the Corinthians to pursue prophecy instead of tongues?

How does this tie in with what we learned about love in the previous chapter?

In Hot Pursuit

Why would pursuing love lend itself more to edifying fellow believers?

What does this passage have in common with 1 Timothy 6:11 and 2 Timothy 2:22?

Based upon your study why would Paul give the instruction to pursue love?

How would you summarize the pursuit of love?

Complete the *Lesson Outline*.

What have you learned about pursuing love?

Complete *My Take on Things*.

Word Summary   Date of Study:

Word:	Verse:_____
Strong's Number:	

Definition:

Times Used: ___ Translated as:

Other Sources	Definition(s)

Other Bible References	How Used

Putting it My Own Words

Takeaway

Love Is

1 Corinthians 13

Verse	Description	Notes- references
1		
2		
3		
4		
5		
6		

What is love?

What did I learn from this chapter?

Love Is

1 Corinthians 13

Verse	Description	Notes- references
7		
8		
9		
10		
11		
12-13		

What is love?

What did I learn from this chapter?

Didactical Summary   Date of Study:

Passage:		Title	
Author:		Thesis:	
Audience:			
Verse	Argument	Statement	Support
Insight			
Takeaway			

Word Summary Date of Study:

Word:	Verse:_____
Strong's Number:	

Definition:

Times Used: ___ Translated as:

Other Sources	Definition(s)

Other Bible References	How Used

Putting it My Own Words

Takeaway

Lesson Outline Summary   Date of Study:

Word:	Title:	
Scripture:	Theme (Context):	

Key Words and phrases

Verse	Points	Support

Takeaway

My Take on Things

My impression
As a result of my study, I discovered and learned something I didn't before
And
And
And
And some more

As a result of my study, I need to work on the following things in my life

I think God wants me to concentrate on:

What is at least one goal I can work toward?

What are the steps I need to take in order to reach my goal?

What kind of timeframe to I wish to accomplish this goal in?

What is the timeframe of the individual steps?

My accountability partner in reaching this goal is
My prayer is
Additional thoughts
Date

Additional Notes:

In Hot Pursuit

...godliness with contentment is great gain

1 Timothy 6:6

Lesson Eight

Pursuing Godliness

Well the good news is we have had such a lovely time exploring 1 Timothy 6 in several previous lessons a lot of our work has already been done! So instead of examining, some of what you will be doing is reviewing. Like bowties and fezzes, reviewing is cool.

Only Whovians will get that. If you don't know who a Whovian is... I feel sorry for you.

I digress!!

In our pursuit of godliness we of course need to define what it is. Luckily, there are only 15 references and they are all in the New Testament. Don't ask why or how come there are none in the Old. I don't know and that is not within the scope of our study. I should also point out that it is used nine times in 1 Timothy 6. That's a clue, BTW.

There are two words for you to consider for this lesson. One is used 14 times and the other only once. Complete the *Word Summaries* for these words.

G2150

G2347

What is your working definition of godliness?

In Hot Pursuit

What did you learn about this word as the result of this study?

Review the notes you already have for 1 timothy 6.

Complete the *Didatical Summary* for 1 Timothy 6.

How many times does Paul use the word godliness in this chapter?

What does he say about godliness in each verse?

1 Timothy 6:3

1 Timothy 6:5

According to this verse what does some people equate with godliness?

1 Timothy 6:6

Complete the *Word Summary* for the word contentment. G841

Why is godliness with contentment great gain?

1 Timothy 6:11

Twelve Things God Wants Us to Know

If you looked at the other mentions of godliness in 1 Timothy, what kind of picture does Paul paint about this topic?

1 Timothy 2:2

1 Timothy 2:10

1 Timothy 3:16 –

What is the mystery of godliness?

1 Timothy 4:7

1 Timothy 4:8

What is the difference between righteousness, godliness and faith and love, patience and gentleness (meekness)? Hint: Galatians 5:22

In Hot Pursuit

According to this passage what does the pursuit of godliness the remedy for?

What are the other commands listed in this passage?

How do these commands relate to the pursuing godliness?

Based upon your study why would Paul give the instruction to pursue godliness?

How would you summarize the pursuit of godliness?

Complete the *Lesson Outline*.

What have you learned about pursuing godliness?

Complete *My Take on Things*.

Word Summary   Date of Study:

Word:	Verse:_____
Strong's Number:	

Definition:

Times Used: _____ Translated as:

Other Sources	Definition(s)

Other Bible References	How Used

Putting it My Own Words

Takeaway

Word Summary Date of Study:

Word:	Verse:_____
Strong's Number:	

Definition:

Times Used: ___ Translated as:

Other Sources	Definition(s)

Other Bible References	How Used

Putting it My Own Words

Takeaway

Didactical Summary

Date of Study:

Passage:		Title		
Author:		Thesis:		
Audience:				
Verse	Argument	Statement		Support
Insight				
Takeaway				

Word Summary Date of Study:

Word:	Verse:_____
Strong's Number:	
Definition:	
Times Used: ___ Translated as:	

Other Sources	Definition(s)

Other Bible References	How Used

Putting it My Own Words

Takeaway

Lesson Outline Summary

Date of Study:

Word:	Title:	
Scripture:	Theme (Context):	
Key Words and phrases		
Verse	Points	Support
Takeaway		

My Take on Things

My impression

As a result of my study, I discovered and learned something I didn't before

And

And

And

And some more

As a result of my study, I need to work on the following things in my life

I think God wants me to concentrate on:
What is at least one goal I can work toward?
What are the steps I need to take in order to reach my goal?
What kind of timeframe to I wish to accomplish this goal in?
What is the timeframe of the individual steps?

My accountability partner in reaching this goal is

My prayer is

Additional thoughts

Date

Additional Notes:

In Hot Pursuit

Therefore let us pursue the things which make for peace and the things by which one may edify another.

Romans 14:19

Lesson Nine

Pursuing Things Which Edify

Well, we have seen this passage before in our journey through the things God wants us to Pursue. That means some of the work has been done already and you have struck it lucky two lessons in a row. Like I said reviewing is cool...

This is one of those words which can be interesting if you are into architecture and building things... 'nuff said.

Let's start where we always start... complete the Word Summary for the word G3619.

What did you discover about the word *edify*?

As part of your study, did you discover any synonyms?

What are they? List the references.

In Hot Pursuit
Review the data you gathered for Romans 14 in Lesson 3.

Verse 19 starts with "let us therefore..." What does usually mean?

Read through the chapter. Does this provide an answer to the question of what things make for edification?

Complete the Survey *Things that Edify*. List the verse, what the thing is and why this would be something which would edify? Be sure to include the complete reference, you may be referring to other passages before you conclude your study.

Are there any other passages which seem to include references to pursuing things?

What are they?

Do you think they could be considered things which edify?

Record them on your Survey.

Why is it important to pursue things which edify?

How would you summarize the pursuit of things which edify?

Complete the *Lesson Outline*.

What have you learned about pursuing things which edify?

Complete *My Take on Things*.

Word Summary   Date of Study:

Word:	Verse:_____
Strong's Number:	

Definition:

Times Used: ___ Translated as:

Other Sources	Definition(s)

Other Bible References	How Used

Putting it My Own Words

Takeaway

Things Which Edify

Verse	What Edifies?	Why Does this Edify

Things Which Edify

Verse	What Edifies?	Why Does this Edify

Lesson Outline Summary

Date of Study:

Word:	Title:	
Scripture:	Theme (Context):	

Key Words and phrases

Verse	Points	Support

Takeaway

My Take on Things

My impression
As a result of my study, I discovered and learned something I didn't before
And
And
And
And some more
As a result of my study, I need to work on the following things in my life

I think God wants me to concentrate on:
What is at least one goal I can work toward?
What are the steps I need to take in order to reach my goal?
What kind of timeframe to I wish to accomplish this goal in?
What is the timeframe of the individual steps?

My accountability partner in reaching this goal is

My prayer is

Additional thoughts

Date

Additional Notes:

In Hot Pursuit

See that no one renders evil for evil to anyone, but always pursue what is good both for yourselves and for all.

1 Thessalonians 5:15

Lesson Ten

Pursuing What is Good

The first thing which came to my mind when I started preparing this lesson was the story where the young man calls Jesus "Good Master." Jesus asked him why he is calling him good since there is none good but God (Matthew 19:16-17; Mark 10:17-18)

Hey that's pretty cool. Jesus is good. God is good. Pursue them and we can end the lesson right here!

Not so fast.

There is always more to the story. I'm not saying you shouldn't pursue Jesus and God (well, they really are the same). That is a very good thing to pursue. But we must consider context. Remember that word? The phrase we are looking at is in 1 Thessalonians 5:15.

So by default we can put Jesus on the top of our list as one of the things God wants us to pursue. But we are still going to examine the passage and discover what other good things God has in mind for us to pursue.

But there is another bonus to this study. Just think. What would have happened if all the good things were listed as things to pursue in themselves? This study would have been a lot longer.

Ok let's start by taking a closer look at the word *good*. Complete your *Word Summary* for G18.

What did you discover when you examined this word?

In Hot Pursuit

Look at the following list of the different ways good can be used. Search the Bible and list a verse which would fit each of the definitions.

1) Of good constitution or nature

2) Useful, salutary

3) Good, pleasant, agreeable, joyful, happy

4) Excellent, distinguished

5) Upright, honorable

Read 1Thessalonians 5:14-22. Before we go into more depth, which definition do you think would best fit the context of the passage?

Why did you make this choice?

Complete the *Didactical Summary* for verses 14-22.

What did you discover about Paul's argument?

This passage starts with the word *now*. So the next question we want to ask is what was he talking about before the now? Usually we are looking for a *then* and are thinking in terms of time or a time line. But this is not necessarily the case. Start by taking a look at verses 11-13.

What was Paul talking about in these verses?

How do you think they would relate to our topic *pursuing what is good*?

What were the things Paul was taking about which they should comfort and edify each other with? Complete the chart *Things Which Comfort and Edify*. Ask yourself if they could relate to our topic and why?

Now let's go back to verses 14-23. Complete the chart *Things Which are Good*.

Why do you think Paul would have added action to these things?

Review the definitions of the word good. After examining 1 Thessalonians 5, have you changed your mind about which definition best fits this context?

If you did, can you explain why you changed your mind? If not did the study reinforce your original decision?

Based upon your study why would you pursue things which are good?

In Hot Pursuit

How would you summarize the pursuit of that which is good?

Complete the *Lesson Outline*.

What have you learned about pursuing that which is good?

Complete *My Take on Things*.

Word Summary   Date of Study:

Word:	Verse:_____
Strong's Number:	
Definition:	
Times Used: ___ Translated as:	

Other Sources	Definition(s)

Other Bible References	How Used

Putting it My Own Words

Takeaway

Didactical Summary   Date of Study:

Passage:		Title	
Author:		Thesis:	
Audience:			
Verse	**Argument**	**Statement**	**Support**

Insight

Takeaway

Things Which Comfort and Edify

Verse	What Comfort and Edifies?	Relates?	Why?
5:10			
9			
8			
7			
6			
5			
4			
3			
2			
1			

Things Which are Good

Verse	What is Good	How	Why?
14			
15			
16			
17			
18			
19			
20			
21			
22			
Any Extra thoughts?			

Lesson Outline Summary   Date of Study:

Word:	Title:	
Scripture:	Theme (Context):	

Key Words and phrases

Verse	Points	Support

Takeaway

My Take on Things

My impression
As a result of my study, I discovered and learned something I didn't before
And
And
And
And some more
As a result of my study, I need to work on the following things in my life

I think God wants me to concentrate on:
What is at least one goal I can work toward?
What are the steps I need to take in order to reach my goal?
What kind of timeframe to I wish to accomplish this goal in?
What is the timeframe of the individual steps?

My accountability partner in reaching this goal is

My prayer is

Additional thoughts

Date

Additional Notes:

In Hot Pursuit

...man of God... pursue... patience.

1 Timothy 6:11

Lesson Eleven

Pursuing Patience

I thought about this old joke when I started working on this lesson. Lord, grant me patience...right now!

Patience is something which seems to be in scarce supply in our society today. Our high speed internet world has created a demand for instant gratification. There is no such thing as waiting. Yet, one of the things God wants us to pursue a quality which is opposite from what we have been trained to accept as the norm.

Before we get into our study ask yourself what is patience. No... Really... Ask yourself this question.

Write down what your definition and understanding of what patience is. When we complete the study I will ask you if you have changed your mind.

Ok now with your definition recorded let's take a closer look at what the Bible has to say about patience and why this is something God wants us to pursue.

Complete the word study for patience – G5281.

In Hot Pursuit
What did you discover about this word?

Here are some other possible meanings for this word. Look at the references were this word is used (there are only 33) and see which definition they fit. If you are not sure about the meaning of these words, you know the drill... reach for a dictionary!

Steadfastness

Constancy

Endurance

Sustaining

Perseverance

Why would these words describe or be associated with *patience*?

Review the notes and observations you have already made about this passage in lessons five – eight. I would add lesson twelve, but that is the next lesson which I'm pretty sure you haven't done yet... unless you have some sort of time-travel device that allowed you to jump ahead and do it.

What is your definition of patience?

Has your understanding of patience changed as a result of your study? Why or why not?

Why do you think Paul instructed Timothy to pursue patience?

Based upon your study why would you pursue patience?

How would you summarize the pursuit of patience?

Complete the *Lesson Outline*.

What have you learned about pursuing patience?

Complete *My Take on Things*.

Word Summary   Date of Study:

Word:	Verse:_____
Strong's Number:	
Definition:	

Times Used: ___ Translated as:	

Other Sources	Definition(s)

Other Bible References	How Used

Putting it My Own Words	

Takeaway	

Lesson Outline Summary

Date of Study:

Word:	Title:	
Scripture:	Theme (Context):	
Key Words and phrases		

Verse	Points	Support
Takeaway		

My Take on Things

My impression
As a result of my study, I discovered and learned something I didn't before
And
And
And
And some more
As a result of my study, I need to work on the following things in my life

I think God wants me to concentrate on:
What is at least one goal I can work toward?
What are the steps I need to take in order to reach my goal?
What kind of timeframe to I wish to accomplish this goal in?
What is the timeframe of the individual steps?

My accountability partner in reaching this goal is

My prayer is

Additional thoughts

Date

Additional Notes:

In Hot Pursuit

…pursue… gentleness

1 Timothy 6:11

Lesson Twelve

Pursuing Gentleness

This is another one of those qualities or characteristics which are not looked on favorably in our society today. Also translated meekness, it is generally viewed as a sign of weakness which is often exploited by others. You may even be thinking along similar lines. The question is why does God want us to pursue something which we may perceive as a liability?

Well, if you have been working in this study with me, I am sure you have been surprised by some of the discoveries you have made. Things aren't always what they seem and before we should jump to conclusions, let's check it out.

Maybe we can put reason to the saying; "Meekness is not the same as weakness."

Complete the *Word Summary* for G4236. Since there are only 9 references where this word is used it would be a good idea to examine all nine. It wouldn't hurt to check out similar words such as meek – G4235 and G4239.

When you have completed your word study fill in the chart *Profile of Meekness*. Make a note if you think the passage can relate to our primary verse and how it relates.

What have you discovered about this word?

In Hot Pursuit

For the final time, review your notes from the five previous lessons were we examined 1 Timothy 6:11.

Based on the context in 1 Timothy 6, why do you think Paul would have included this quality as one God wants us to pursue?

In your journey through this topic, was there any reference made to this being a quality demonstrated by Jesus? List the reference and what the passage was about.

Do you think of Jesus as a weak person? Why or why not?

Based upon your study why would you pursue gentleness?

How would you summarize the pursuit of gentleness?

Complete the *Lesson Outline*.

What have you learned about pursuing gentleness?

Complete *My Take on Things*.

Word Summary   Date of Study:

Word:	Verse:_____
Strong's Number:	
Definition:	
Times Used: ___ Translated as:	

Other Sources	Definition(s)

Other Bible References	How Used

Putting it My Own Words

Takeaway

Word Summary   Date of Study:

Word:	Verse:_____
Strong's Number:	
Definition:	
Times Used: ___ Translated as:	

Other Sources	Definition(s)

Other Bible References	How Used

Putting it My Own Words	

Takeaway	

Word **Summary** Date of Study:

Word:	Verse:_____
Strong's Number:	
Definition:	
Times Used: ___ Translated as:	

Other Sources	Definition(s)

Other Bible References	How Used

Putting it My Own Words

Takeaway

Profile of Meekness

Verse or Passage	What do we learn?	Does it relate?	How does it relate?
What I've discovered about meekness is...			

Profile of Meekness

Verse or Passage	What do we learn?	Does it relate?	How does it relate?
What I've discovered about meekness is…			

Profile of Meekness

Verse or Passage	What do we learn?	Does it relate?	How does it relate?
What I've discovered about meekness is…			

Lesson Outline Summary

Date of Study:

Word:	Title:	
Scripture:	Theme (Context):	
Key Words and phrases		
Verse	Points	Support
Takeaway		

My Take on Things

My impression
As a result of my study, I discovered and learned something I didn't before
And
And
And
And some more

As a result of my study, I need to work on the following things in my life

I think God wants me to concentrate on:

What is at least one goal I can work toward?

What are the steps I need to take in order to reach my goal?

What kind of timeframe to I wish to accomplish this goal in?

What is the timeframe of the individual steps?

My accountability partner in reaching this goal is

My prayer is

Additional thoughts

Date

Additional Notes:

Not that I have already attained, or am already perfected; but I press on, that I may lay hold of that for which Christ Jesus has also laid hold of me.

Philippians 3:14

Lesson Thirteen

Pursuing That for Which I was Pursued

Just when you thought you were going to wind down this study with something easy along comes this teaser. What is Paul Talking about here? What is he attempting to lay hold of that which Christ has also laid hold of him?

That is why we are committed to doing this study.

You know, it may not be as hard as you think. After all we have the context of Philippians 3 to fall back on.

Let's start our study by doing our Word Summary of G2638

What did you discover about this word?

Complete the Verse Summaries for verses 7 – 14.

When looking over your verse summaries, do you see any pattern in the words Paul is using to describe his goal?

In Hot Pursuit

What is the pattern?

What are the words which describe this pattern? List the verses where the words are.

Now going back over these verses, follow Paul's argument and recorded it on the Didactical Summary.

How is Paul describing his pursuit of Jesus?

What is Paul's attitude?

Think about what Jesus did for us. How is this similar to what Paul is describing for himself?

Did Jesus give up everything to save us?

What did He give up? List verses to support your conclusions.

Complete the comparison chart Jesus vs. Paul. Be sure to include the verses you use to support your conclusions.

What insights did you arrive at as a result of this comparison study?

How would you summarize this pursuit?

In Hot Pursuit
Complete the *Lesson Outline*.

What have you learned about pursuing Christ the way he pursued you?

Complete *My Take on Things*.

Word Summary   Date of Study:

Word:	Verse:_____
Strong's Number:	
Definition:	
Times Used: ___ Translated as:	
Other Sources	**Definition(s)**
Other Bible References	**How Used**
Putting it My Own Words	
Takeaway	

Verse Summary

Date of Study:

Title:	
Verse:	
Strong's Number and Definition(s)	**Used Elsewhere**
Quotation? Yes No	**Summary of Original Passage**
Summary of Verse in Context	
Putting it in My Own Words	
Takeaway	

Verse Summary

Date of Study:

Title:	
Verse:	
Strong's Number and Definition(s)	**Used Elsewhere**
Quotation? Yes No	**Summary of Original Passage**
Summary of Verse in Context	
Putting it in My Own Words	
Takeaway	

Verse Summary Date of Study:

Title:	
Verse:	
Strong's Number and Definition(s)	**Used Elsewhere**
Quotation? Yes No	**Summary of Original Passage**
Summary of Verse in Context	
Putting it in My Own Words	
Takeaway	

Verse Summary Date of Study:

Title:	
Verse:	
Strong's Number and Definition(s)	**Used Elsewhere**
Quotation? Yes No	**Summary of Original Passage**
Summary of Verse in Context	
Putting it in My Own Words	
Takeaway	

Verse Summary Date of Study:

Title:	
Verse:	
Strong's Number and Definition(s)	**Used Elsewhere**
Quotation? Yes No	**Summary of Original Passage**
Summary of Verse in Context	
Putting it in My Own Words	
Takeaway	

Verse Summary Date of Study:

Title:	
Verse:	
Strong's Number and Definition(s)	**Used Elsewhere**
Quotation? Yes No	**Summary of Original Passage**
Summary of Verse in Context	
Putting it in My Own Words	
Takeaway	

Verse Summary Date of Study:

Title:	
Verse:	
Strong's Number and Definition(s)	**Used Elsewhere**
Quotation? Yes No	**Summary of Original Passage**
Summary of Verse in Context	
Putting it in My Own Words	
Takeaway	

Verse Summary

Date of Study:

Title:	
Verse:	
Strong's Number and Definition(s)	**Used Elsewhere**
Quotation? Yes No	**Summary of Original Passage**
Summary of Verse in Context	
Putting it in My Own Words	
Takeaway	

Comparison Summary

Jesus vs. Paul

Jesus gave up...	Scripture	Paul gave up...

Insight:

Takeway:

Lesson Outline Summary

Date of Study:

Word:	Title:
Scripture:	Theme (Context):

Key Words and phrases

Verse	Points	Support

Takeaway

My Take on Things

My impression

As a result of my study, I discovered and learned something I didn't before

And

And

And

And some more

As a result of my study, I need to work on the following things in my life

I think God wants me to concentrate on:
What is at least one goal I can work toward?
What are the steps I need to take in order to reach my goal?
What kind of timeframe to I wish to accomplish this goal in?
What is the timeframe of the individual steps?

My accountability partner in reaching this goal is

My prayer is

Additional thoughts

Date

Additional Notes:

In Hot Pursuit

As the deer pants for the water brooks, So pants my soul for You, O God.

Psalm 42:1

Snapshots and Wrap up

We are coming to the end of our journey together exploring the things God wants us to pursue. I hope you have been as blessed as I have been by this study. I pray you have been challenged by your time in the Bible to strive to convert your knowledge into action.

But I'm not going to let you get away that easily.

This chapter is a snapshot of your study here. I could have called it a review... but you would have stopped reading at this point and close the book.

As you review each lesson I would like you to create a snapshot of each thing we are to pursue. This is not a complete in depth exercise but only of the highlights of the study. In other words you are creating a snapshot that you can use as a refresher of your time in this study.

Thank you for traveling with me in this study. I hope we get a chance to meet again.

Keep looking up!

Steve

God wants me to pursue...

What?	Passage(s)
Key Ideas?	
What I learned...	
Why I should pursue this	

What?	Passage(s)
Key Ideas?	
What I learned...	
Why I should pursue this	

God wants me to pursue…

What?	Passage(s)

Key Ideas?

What I learned…

Why I should pursue this

What?	Passage(s)

Key Ideas?

What I learned…

Why I should pursue this

God wants me to pursue...

What?	Passage(s)
Key Ideas?	
What I learned...	
Why I should pursue this	

What?	Passage(s)
Key Ideas?	
What I learned...	
Why I should pursue this	

God wants me to pursue...

What?	Passage(s)
Key Ideas?	
What I learned...	
Why I should pursue this	

What?	Passage(s)
Key Ideas?	
What I learned...	
Why I should pursue this	

God wants me to pursue...

What?	Passage(s)
Key Ideas?	
What I learned...	
Why I should pursue this	

What?	Passage(s)
Key Ideas?	
What I learned...	
Why I should pursue this	

God wants me to pursue...

What?	Passage(s)

Key Ideas?

What I learned...

Why I should pursue this

What?	Passage(s)

Key Ideas?

What I learned...

Why I should pursue this

Bonus Studies

The following are experts from:

 The Bible School Dropout's Bigger and Better Guide to Bible Study (2008)

The Bible School Dropout's Guide to More Bible Study (2010)

The Topical Study for a Change of Pace

One of the things we have learned in our study to this point is inductive Bible study is very applicable to studying books of the Bible. You start with chapter one, verse one and go from there. But how do we take this information and apply it to other types of studies, where there is not just one passage to examine, but several. What do we do? How do we approach it?

Well, aren't you lucky! Now we are going to take a look at how to apply this method to other types of studies. This particular lesson will take you through the steps of studying what God's word has to say about a single subject. And we are going to do using the same 5 little words we have been using; who, what, where, when, why, and how. Actually that's six...

Our objective is to find out what God has to say about a subject. We want to set our mind on asking the right question: What does the Bible have to say about......

A mistake many people have is to start out on this study thinking: I believe this, or my friends believe that, or my church or minister teaches this. You, your friends, your church and your minister are not the final authorities on a subject. The Bible is.

Our study today is to look at a topic that while in many of today's religious groups is a minor thing, which you can take it or leave it, others consider it a sacred duty which needs to be performed in order to gain God's grace. That is the Lord's Supper.

You may be asking, "What about the rest of 1 Peter?"

There are a lot of subjects, or topics in 1 Peter we could focus on and keep very busy learning all we can. Since we are changing gears, I thought it would be nice to look at something not related to 1 Peter. So, we'll give his letter a break; we've been picking on him for a while. Besides, there is enough material in first and second Peter for another book. Now, back to the Lord's Supper....

In Hot Pursuit

"Why this topic?" You ask? I'm the one writing the book. When you write your book on Bible Study, you get to choose the topics you want to cover. This one happens to be a favorite of mine.

Depending on your religious orientation, The Lord's Supper is also called The Eucharist, Communion, The Lord's Table, or Breaking of Bread. You or your church may never observe it, observe it only once a year, once a month, weekly or daily. There are groups who believe the elements are symbolic and those who believe they are transformed into the blood and body of Christ. Who is right? What view is correct?

Let's take a look at what the Bible has to say.

Just the Facts, Ma'am

What to do? What to do? Where to start? When we approach a topical study, the first thing to realize is the topic we are covering is probably not in one spot in the Bible. So we get out our dusty....er....trusty concordance again and start to look up the passages we have which refer to our topic. We start by looking at the first reference and then moving on from there. If you find hundreds of verses related to your topic, then you make a choice of including every passage in your study, or get enough of a sampling that you are fairly confident you can arrive at a correct conclusion.

We already have some of the tools we need to begin our study. They are the charts that have already been discussed in this book. There will be a few more in the lessons to come which will also be useful in discovering what the Bible has to say on this subject.

Since this is a new type of study, I'll cut you a break this time. I'll give you the references where you will find mention of this topic.

Matthew 26:26-30

Mark 14:22-26

Luke 22:14-20

Acts 2:42-46

Acts 20:7-12

1 Corinthians 10:15-22

Corinthians 11: 20-30.

Now we make some observations of these verses in their context. What are the events surrounding these passages? Who are the people involved? Where did this take place? Is there any indication why it occurred? If you are not partial to notebooks and want to use the Observation Summaries, that is fine.

When we look at the passages in Matthew, Mark, Luke, and 1 Corinthians 11, we discover they all record the same event, from the perspective of four men. These are called parallel references and by looking at them, we get a picture of the night Jesus started this observance.

The passages in Acts and 1 Corinthians 10 are conceptual references. These two refer to the Lord's Supper, Breaking of Bread. The passages in Acts tells us the disciples practiced it everyday at first and then once a week as the Church spread out into the world. 1 Corinthians addresses people's attitudes when gathering together and what this meal means on a spiritual level.

You may also discover there are passages which refer to your topic, but make no direct reference to it. These are implied passages. For instance, Jesus tells the disciples the cup of wine represents His blood of the New Covenant. The New Covenant is first mentioned in Jeremiah 31:31-34. It is important to look at this passage as it ties in with the events of the evening. Having an understanding of what the Passover is and its significance is also important to understanding the Lord's Supper.

Go over your notes and make a list of the similarities and differences. Look for repeated words, concepts, or contrasts. These will provide you with your key words and phrases. Does this sound familiar?

Absolutely! It was this in Lesson two. This isn't a totally new process, just building on what you have learned.

The first thing to do is make some observations. Looking at the passages, you can list the players. What they were doing and what they were saying. Develop a list of repeated words and phrases. You get to do this part as well.

My List of Words and Phrases	Your List of Words and Phrases
Took bread Blessed it Broke it Take eat, this is my body Took the cup Gave thanks My blood of the new covenant Won't do it again until the Father's kingdom comes Communion, and fellowship Breaking bread Do this in remembrance of me	

Breaking it Down

After the overview, the next step is to break it down and take a look at the components of the stories. You want to make note of the similarities of the accounts as well as the differences. This helps to give an overview. Also, you want to look at how our keys were used. For instance, there are a couple of interesting metaphors in these accounts. Jesus indicated the bread represented His body and the wine His blood. But they also signified something else. They were a remembrance of His sacrifice and the covenant which He instituted with His death.

Breaking it Down	Key words, ideas and explanations
bread ' body Luke and Paul added "which is given for you, Do this in remembrance of me"	remembrance ' a recollection, a memorial, or a commemoration - Luke 22:19; 1 Cor. 11:24-25; Heb. 10:3 -remembering His sacrifice. -proclaiming His death (1 Cor 11:26) -modern Passover the *tzafun or afikomen, eaten at the end of the meal*

From your observations, you should also have developed a list of questions to continue your investigation. There are probably some more, but here is a start.

1.   What is Passover?
2.   What is the New Covenant?

3. What are we remembering?
4. What is the significance of Jesus saying He will not partake of the fruit of the vine until He is in the Father's kingdom with them?
5. What does breaking of bread mean?
6. What are we doing when we observe the Lord's Supper?
7. Does the Bible give any indication on how this is done?
8. Does the Bible give any indication on how often this is done?

In the differences between the accounts Matthew and Mark, for instance wrote that when Jesus gave the bread to the Disciples he said. "Take, eat; this is my body." Luke and Paul record Christ's words as *"This is my body which is given for you; do this in remembrance of Me."*

Of the four writers, only Matthew was at the event. It appears Mark may have used Matthew or even the other disciples as the source for his letter. Luke may have used different sources and Paul and Luke worked together. So the good doctor was probably one Paul's source. However, the question comes up that one or more of the writers were wrong.

No. It means writers are talking about the same events from their unique viewpoints and what they wanted to emphasize. Based on your study, you will be able to decide how everything fits together.

Take a look at the context of the passages. What was happening during this time? Does any other Scripture record the events of that night? Do other Scriptures demonstrate the disciples observing the Lord's Supper?

Now that you concluded your observations and worked at understanding the various passages in context, the next step is to create an overview of what you learned. Part of the overview is to recap your observations and to provide answers to some of the questions that were posed in the early part of the study. If other charts were used in the study, that information should also be used in creating the overview. It should also answer the question as to what the Lord's supper is and why we observe it.

As with all of your studies, you want to record what we learned at the conclusion of the study. What did you takeaway from the study? Was there something new that was brought to light, or are you seeing this service in a different light? These are some of the questions that should be considered.

In Hot Pursuit
Organizing Our Study

As with previous lessons, you want to organize the study into a logical fashion or into an outline. The format is similar to the outlines created in lesson eight. However, instead of organizing a chapter, which is already a unit, starting from verse one to the end of the chapter, you are dealing with multiple passages.

When it comes to organizing the outline, the questions is where to start. There are several different options depending on what we want to emphasize. The outline can be based on the first mention of the topic, by the passage. It can also be organize chronologically (time), historically (events) or topically (key words and phrases). Develop the theme and main points of your study and then the supporting statements or points under each of the main points. Working this way keeps the study consistent. It may be useful to create a couple of outlines, looking at the subject from different perspectives.

The following are some examples of the main points of different outlines based on different perspectives.

Scripture

A.   Matthew wrote:
B.   Mark wrote:
C.   Luke wrote:
D.   Paul wrote:

Chronological

A.   The night before the cross.
B.   After the Passover meal.
C.   When the Church gathers.
D.   Until Jesus comes.

Historical

A.   Passover: A remembrance of national deliverance.
B.   Passover: The last meal before the cross.
C.   Passover: A remembrance of spiritual deliverance.
D.   Passover: Faith shall be sight.

Topical

A.   Remembrance

A.   Blessing
B.   Thanksgiving
C.   New Covenant
D.   Fellowship
E.   Proclamation
F.   Participation
G.   Anticipation

Here is an example of a topical-topical outline (uh... subject-topical, topical-subject? Your guess is a good as mine.) Included with the point are the sub points, the verses the points came from as well as supporting cross references.

In Hot Pursuit

Verse	Points	Cross References
Matt 26:26 Mark 14:22 Luke 22:19 1 Cor 11:24-25	1. A Memorial 1.1 a physical reminder 1.2 His sacrifice 1.3 the shedding of His blood 1.4 the price paid for my salvation	Joshua 4:1-7 1 Peter 1:18

Finally, what was the point of the study? As with all of our other studies, we want to wrap it up with the takeaway. Has our perspective changed from the beginning of the study to the end? Have our eyes been opened the reason and importance of this simple service? What does it represent and does it deserve to be a 15 minute addendum at the end of the service on the first Sunday of the month? What are your conclusions on the matter?

Wrappin' it Up

With this lesson, we built upon our study methods to add how to approach a topic or single subject instead of a chapter unit. Instead at looking primarily at one passage of Scripture, we learned how to look at multiple passages relating to the same thing. We applied the same observation techniques that we learned earlier to come up with a list of the key words, phrases and idea.

By comparing similarities, differences, looking at the words, historical references, and such, we were able to get a complete overview of our subject. From that we could make objective conclusions and arrive at a takeaway which is consistent with what we have studied.

I deliberately chose a topic which was limited in the scope of verses which referred to it. Otherwise we would have been spending a lot more than this one lesson could cover. It doesn't matter what subject you are interested in, the steps remain basically the same. Whether you are interested in studying the grace of God, mercy, salvation, atonement, or something else, the basic steps are the same.

The next lesson will take the concepts we learned and apply them to a person or a biographical study. We can learn a lot from the people of the Bible in their character, what they did, or didn't do, and their relationship with God. We are going to meet an interesting young woman named Mary B.

The Fun and Profit of Word Studies

I saw a film which started looking down on the head of a person at a distance of one meter (39 inches for our American friends) away. Every few seconds, the camera backed up by a factor of ten: ten meters, 100 meters, 1,000 meters, ten-thousand meters.

You saw the person, the ground around him. Then the nearby structures came into view. Soon you were zooming through the clouds and the earth came into view. As you moved faster outward, planets sailed past, then the stars. Finally, you saw the Milky Way and the universe. Come to think of it, I wonder if we will see the same thing when the Rapture happens!

The camera reversed direction and we closed in again on our galaxy. Passing the stars and planets again, we see earth come again into view and enter the atmosphere, ending at the place we started.

From there it decreased in distance to the skin by the same factor of ten; 1 meter (100 centimeters), 10 centimeters, 1 centimeter, 1 decimeter, 1 millimeter. The camera closed in on the skin, the hair follicles and the texture of the skin. The camera kept going into the skin. It showed the cell, its interior, the nucleus, right down to the DNA and the molecules that formed it.

The View backed out until the camera was at the place it began.

Inductive Bible study is a lot like that. We work to see the big picture. What the book is about, its theme(s) and what the writer was attempting to communicate to his audience. But to get to see the whole picture, it is necessary to take a look at all the small parts that make up the whole. The small parts in a Bible study are the words. What did these words mean to the original audience? Is there only one meaning, or are there multiple meanings?

We also have to take into consideration the fact the original Bible was not written in English (that may come as a shock to a few people), but in 3 different language. So we are working through translators who attempted to interpret it in a way that was as close to the original as possible.

In Hot Pursuit

There are also meanings of words which often don't relate directly to the basic meaning of the word, but have cultural significance to it which doesn't make sense to people unfamiliar to the language.

In a word study we pull out our microscope and look in detail at the words which make up the passage we are studying. You will be amazed at what you discover!

Let's take a fairly well-known verse; 2 Timothy 2:15. *"Be diligent to present yourself approved to God, a worker who does not need to be ashamed, rightly dividing the word of truth."*

On the surface, this seems pretty straightforward. To study meant to stick my nose in a book and learn. By learning I was showing myself approved to God. Because I had learned God's Word, I would not be ashamed handling it. In other words, I wouldn't look like a horse's .... uh, be embarrassed by my ignorance. My wife's best friend said the first time she taught Sunday school, she told the kids that Jesus had every bone in His body broken when He was crucified. I don't know about your Bible, but that tidbit of information isn't in my version.

When you study the words, you are looking for a base definition and its connotations, or other meanings. It is also important to learn of any cultural or historical significance attached to the word. Was it used in an idiomatic sense, which usually doesn't make any sense when translated directly? For instance when we say we've got our ducks lined up, we don't mean real ducks trained to stand at attention, but that we have everything in order.

Even the cultures of the Bibles had idiomatic references. An example is Rom 3:4 *"Certainly not! Indeed, let God be true but every man a liar. As it is written..."* The phrase "certainly not" is literally "let it be not." However, it is considered an idiom and has be translated as "Not on your life! Depend on it (MSG)," "God forbid (KJV)," "Certainly not! (EMTV)," "Absolutely not! (ALT)." Of course, you could be using today's idiomatic phrase: "Let it be. NOT!"

By looking at various definitions of the word, we can gain a totally different perspective on the old chestnuts many of us memorized in Sunday School.

Getting back to 2 Timothy 2:16. Here is the verse after I had completed a word study. *"Be diligent, earnest and eager to present or exhibit yourself tried and approved, as refined metal is purified by fire, to God, a laborer irreproachable, having no cause to be ashamed, skillfully and correctly handling and teaching the word of truth."*

This goes like, way totally beyond the Daily Bread[1], those ready made study guides in the bookstore, or our morning quiet time. Not that those things are not important, they are. But this verse doesn't talk about cracking the Book and burning the midnight oil.

What it does talk about is working hard towards a goal. That goal is to gain God's approval in the work we do (Mattewh 25:21). It also brings in the aspect of testing and trials we experience on our spiritual journey (1 Peter 1:7; James 1:2-3). This verse speaks of is maturity and the ability to teach others (2 Timothy 2:2; Hebrew 4:11-14). This verse also addresses our attitude and responsibility towards God (Romans 1:16; 1 Peter 3:16-17).

Why you could preach a sermon on just this verse. There is even the base of an outline for you to expand upon and present you message to your appreciative audience.

It will be these times of digging deep into God's word your jaw will drop with amazement and you will drop on your knees in praise and thanksgiving, or in conviction and repentance. You will laugh and cry as the Holy Spirit reveals truths to you in a way you have never thought possible. You will grow in the grace and knowledge of God and our Lord Jesus Christ.

Doing a word study still uses the principles of inductive Bible study. We are still working on our three stages, observation, interpretation, and application, although this is moving into the interpretation phase of our study. What did this mean to the original audience and how do we bridge the gap between the first century and the 21st?

Learning to "Speak" the Language

Let's take a look at our friend, Peter. Back in lesson 2, one of the observations we made was that He was an apostle. Naturally the next question is: What's an apostle? Many of us have an idea of whom or what an apostle may be, but do we know what the term meant to those people to whom Peter wrote?

---

[1]Daily Bread is a respected publication produced by RBC Ministries, Grand Rapids, MI

In Hot Pursuit

So, how do we go about reaching our goal? Very few of us have a working knowledge of Koiné (The commonly spoken Greek dialect). However there were and are some very capable theologians who do and have created some wonderful tools to help us understand the original languages.

James Strong, a theologian in the 1800's, had a fascination for the words in the Bible. He wrote a book called a concordance. He made a list of every word in the Bible and every verse it's in. Now, if that isn't cool enough, after all, he did this without the aid of a word processor, he gave each of these words a number which correspond to the Greek work which was used. So by looking up the number, you were able to get the basic meanings of the word in the Greek language.

So we open our online Bible, or pull out the trusty book and look up the word "apostle."

Besides a list of references, we see the number 652. Now by clicking on the link, or going to the Greek-English dictionary in the back of the Concordance, we look up the number to the corresponding word. When we find the number, we get this entry:

apostolos

apostolos

ap-os'-tol-os

From G649; a *delegate*; specifically an *ambassador* of the Gospel; officially a *commissioner* of Christ ("apostle"), (with miraculous powers): - apostle, messenger, he that is sent.[2]

That is a nice working definition, but do we have enough information about how the word was used by the people in everyday, normal usage. No. So we look for more information.

Another theologian of approximately the same time, create a dictionary of biblical words. W.E. vine listed the English words and then provided the Greek words and definitions that are translated into the Word:

APOSTLE, APOSTLESHIP

1. *apostolos* (apostolos) is, lit., one sent forth (*apo*, from, *stello*, to send). The word is used of the Lord Jesus to describe His relation to God, Heb. 3:1; see John 17:3. The twelve disciples chosen by the Lord for special training were so called,

---

[2]James Strong, *The New Strong's Complete Dictionary of Bible Words,* (Nashville: Thomas Nelson Publishers, 1996) 585

Luke 6:13; 9:10. Paul, though he had seen the Lord Jesus, 1 Cor. 9:1; 15:8, had not companied with the Twelve all the time of His earthly ministry, and hence was not eligible for a place among them, according to Peters description of the necessary qualifications, Acts 1:22. Paul was commissioned directly, by the Lord Himself, after His Ascension, to carry the gospel to the Gentiles.

The word has also a wider reference. In Acts 14:4, 14, it is used of Barnabas as well as of Paul; in Rom. 16:7 of Andronicus and Junias. In 2 Cor. 8:23 (RV, margin) two unnamed brethren are called apostles of the churches; in Phil. 2:25 (RV, margin) Epaphroditus is referred to as your apostle. It is used in 1 Thess. 2:6 of Paul, Silas and Timothy, to define their relation to Christ.

2. *apostole* (, 651), a sending, a mission, signifies an apostleship, Acts 1:25; Rom. 1:5; 1 Cor. 9:2; Gal. 2:8.

Note: Pseudapostoloi, false apostles, occurs in 2 Cor. 11:13.[3]

Well, know that's more like it. The more information, the better. This gives us a clearer understanding of how this word is used.

More contemporary to our time is Spiros Zodhiates. His work, *The Complete Word Study Dictionary: New Testament*, uses the Strong's numbering system. So you look up the number and he gives you the definition. And what a definition it is! He attempts to provide how a particular word is used in context to the passage used. Here is a sample:

....one sent, apostle, ambassador. Sometimes used syn, with *presbeutés,* ambassador (2 Cor 5:20; Eph 6:20). The messenger or ambassador...can never be greater than the one who sent him....The Lord chose the term apóstoloi to indicate the distinctive relation of the Twelve Apostles whom He chose.....designates the office as instituted by Christ...also designates the authority which those called....possess... Paul justified ...being counted as an apostle....he had been called to the office by Christ...

...from the very beginning....applied in a much wider sense to all who ministered as colleagues of the Twelve...

...no continuity of office...no place were instructed to ordain...

---

[3]W.E. Vine, *A Comprehensive Dictionary of the Original Greek Words with their Precise Meanings for English Readers.* (McLean: MacDonald Publishing Company) 65

In Hot Pursuit
      ...applied to Christ... [4]

Kind of makes you want to run right out and get your own copy.

Other sources can give us information like how many times the word is used and how it is translated. This particular word was used 81 times in the New Testament. 78 times it was translated *apostle,* twice as *messenger* and once as *he who is sent*.[5]

If you can, you can also take a look at similar words. For instance Strong's 651, *apostolé commission*, that is, (specifically) *apostolate:* - apostleship. and 649 apostellᴖ *set apart*, that is, (by implication) to *send out* (properly on a mission) literally or figuratively: - put in, send (away, forth, out), set [at liberty]. This could be considered in your observations.

Taking a Walk Thru the Bible

Now that you have a definition, the next step is to start looking up the passages to see how the word is used in the various contexts. Although looking at all of the verses is ideal, sometimes it is used so often is not practical to do so. However if you examine enough of them, you will get to the same place. Don't forget to record what you discover and how it is used. When this is done, you will be able to create what I call a working definition. You have a complete picture of what an apostle is, what the office is about, the qualifications of an apostle and what role he played in the early church.

This gives you a partial picture of who Peter is and the authority he has to speak on behalf of Jesus Christ. If you want to discover more about why Peter was qualified to write what he did, you can study the other titles he called himself, *elder, witness, and partaker*. For this lesson, we'll pretend that we did.

Take a look at the following verses (I promise the list will be there...) and make a note of what they have to say about apostles. Record what you find on the Word Summary. The verses we look at will fit into one of three categories: Directly relevant, indirectly relevant and not relevant.

Allow me to explain, before some of you get the idea that parts of the Bible are relevant and parts aren't. Since we are studying the word Aapostle@ in relation to Peter, any verses we look at which refer to Peter would be directly relevant to our study. Verses which talk about the Apostles, but not directly referring to Peter are indirectly relevant. They are important to our

---

[4]Spiros Zodhiates, *The Complete Word Study Dictionary, New Testament*, (Chattanooga: AMG Publishers, 1992) 238

[5]*The New Strong's Dictionary of Hebrew and Greek Words,* electronic , Libronix Digital Library System 2.0

study as they give us insight to what an Apostle is and does. The third list is those references which are not relevant to our study.

The directly relevant passages would be Acts 2:37 or 8:14. They refer to Peter as his role as an apostle. Verses like Mark 6:30, Acts 2:43 and Jude 17 refer to Apostles in general. Verses like 2 Corinthians 8:23 and Philippians 2:25 use the word apostle in its everyday, normal usage "messenger," and do not refer to either Peter or the other Apostles. These are examples of passages that are not relevant to our study.

The List (finally!)

Acts 5:18	Romans 1:1	Galatians 1:1
Acts 5:29	Romans 11:13	Galatians 1:17
Acts 5:34	Romans 16:7	Galatians 1:19
Acts 5:40	1 Corinthians 1:1	Ephesians 1:1
Acts 6:6	1 Corinthians 4:9	Ephesians 2:20
Acts 8:1	1 Corinthians 9:1	Ephesians 3:5
Acts 8:14	1 Corinthians 9:2	Ephesians 4:11
Acts 8:18	1 Corinthians 9:5	Philippians 2:25
Acts 9:27	1 Corinthians 12:28	Colossians 1:1
Acts 11:1	1 Corinthians 12:29	1 Thessalonians 2:6
Acts 14:4	1 Corinthians 15:7	1 Timothy 1:1
Acts 14:14	1 Corinthians 15:9	1 Timothy 2:7
Acts 15:2	2 Corinthians 1:1	
Acts 15:4	2 Corinthians 8:23	
Acts 15:6	2 Corinthians 11:5	
Acts 15:22	2 Corinthians 11:13	
Acts 15:23	2 Corinthians 12:11	
Acts 15:33	2 Corinthians 12:12	
Acts 16:4		

Even though I did not include them here, you should also consider looking at any synonyms of this word you find. These include Strong's 649 *apostolé* which means 'apostleship" or "commission," and 651 *apostello*, - to send.

We have sifted through all of this information, and have drawn some conclusions. We have an understanding of how the word was used, the context it was used in, and what it meant to the original audience. We create a working definition which we can apply to our study.

What did we learn?

- Generally, an apostle is a messenger or ambassador representing someone
- They were the 12 specifically chosen by Christ to be his messengers and an office was created to mark their position and authority
- Paul is considered an Apostle because he was personally called by Jesus
- They showed their authority with signs and wonders
- They formed the foundation of the Church and laid out the doctrine/teaching of the Church
- Those people who worked with/for the Apostles were often given the same designation, but did not have the authority or the designation of the office.

Now we want to take what we learn and apply it directly to Peter in the context of our study. We have gathered enough information and have correctly interpreted the passage we can put our conclusions into our own words.

- Peter was one of the 12 chosen by Christ and trained by Him to help found and establish the Church and set its direction
- He is uniquely qualified to address these concerns, having experienced persecution first hand
- He is also an eye witness to the glory of Jesus and the grace given by God and is able to testify to that fact. He experienced this when he was the transfiguration.
- His authority to speak comes directly from Jesus

We have examined this particular word, discovered it base meaning, connotations and idiomatic usage. To the best of our knowledge, we have come to an understanding on what is meant to the people Peter was writing to. Did you learn anything significant? What did you takeaway from your study here? How does this information pertain to the letter he wrote and what should be our response to it?

The Building Blocks

In a way, Understanding how to do a word study is probably one of the more important studies that you will learn in this book. Words are the building blocks of the sentences which convey the thoughts of the inspired writers to their audience and ultimately to us. By knowing the base meanings and connotations of the words in their original languages often clears up questions we may have when we work to understand the English words in our Bibles. Sometimes, when we take a closer look, we come up with a different perspective then when we started.

Take a look at the following words and using your tools, find out what they would have meant to the people Peter was writing to. To make it a little easier, I've included the Strong's number.

1 Peter 1:5 - kept (5432)

1 Peter 1:18 - conversation (391)

1 Peter 2:6 - confounded (2617)

1 Peter 2:9 - peculiar (4047)

1 Peter 4:4 - excess (401)

1 Peter 4:8 - charity (26)

Takin' it to Go.

In this lesson, we learned how to discover the base meaning of the word, its connotations and idiomatic, everyday usage. By understanding what it would have meant to the people in their culture, we can gain an understanding why a particular word was used in the context of the passage we are studying.

We learn how it is used by looking up the references where it appears and looking at in that context. This gives a bigger picture of the word.

We also learned that by being able to put it into our own words, we are better able to reach a valid conclusion and taking away a spiritual principle.

In Hot Pusuit

The next lesson goes hand in hand with this one. We will be applying what we learned here to an entire verse and being able to create our own paraphrase.

A Poem by any Other Name

It is often said that art is in the eye of the beholder. I've seen some art that wouldn't behold in my eyes as art and yet they are considered masterpieces.

One example in Canada which raised eyebrows, was a painting purchased by the National Art Gallery of Canada. This "work of art" was nothing more than a blue canvas with a red stripe painted down the middle. The name of the painting; *Voice of Fire*." It created a firestorm all right. The purchase cost several million taxpayer dollars. There was much criticism about the waste of taxpayers' money when anybody with a paint brush and two cans of latex paint could have done the same thing for under a couple of hundred bucks. The curators of the art museum vigorously defended their choice and the furor eventually died down.

The moral of the story is this: Don't buy with other people's money what you wouldn't buy for yourself! And of course P.T. Barnum's famous comment, "There's a sucker born every minute," fits the bill, too!

Poetry is to the literary world what art is to the visual world. It expresses the highest thoughts and deepest emotions of humans. As a result, the author often uses highly imaginative or figurative language to convey those thoughts.

When we think of poetry, the first thing that comes to mind is it rhymes and follows a rhythmic pattern of speech.

Roses are red

Violets are Blue

Sugar is sweet,

But not as sweet as you.

In Hot Pusuit

Hebrew authors did not use this style of writing in their poetry. As common to many eastern cultures, the poetry was written more to provoke the human intellect and make the audience consider the words of the writer.

Instead of a rhythmic pattern, most Hebrew poetry was written in a parallel or symmetrical pattern. The author states a though in the first line and then restates it in the second line.

Each line is called a stitch or a colon. The couplet formed is called a distitch.

Proverbs 1:20

"Wisdom calls aloud outside;

She raises her voice in the open square"

If the author carried his though over into a third line, then the form is called a tristitch.

Psalm 1:1

"Blessed is the man

Who walks not in the counsel of the ungodly

Nor stands in the path of sinners,

Nor sits in the seat of the scornful;"

Hebrew poetry rarely added a fourth line. Perhaps the author said all he had to say in 3 lines and wasn't interested in creating a quad-stitch; or maybe a cross-stitch.

When you read Job, Psalms, Proverbs, Song of Solomon, Ecclesiastes, and Lamentations, you will notice this pattern. It doesn't mean the author was drinking and forgot what he had just written, but that was the form in which they expressed their thoughts.

You may be surprised to know that this form wasn't only limited to poetry and songs. About half of the Hebrew Old Testament is written in a similar manner.6

Take a look at Genesis 1:1-2 where you can see a parallel idea presented.

"In the beginning God created the heavens and the earth.

The earth was without form, and void; and darkness was on the face of the deep. And the Spirit of God was hovering over the face of the waters."

Even when you compare Genesis chapters one and two, you see the author repeats some of the details of the first chapter and goes into greater detail of what happened on the sixth day.

You can classify parallelisms several ways. The first is the author is basically restating the first though in the second line. This is called *synonymous parallelism.*

Psalm 2:4

"He who sits in the heavens shall laugh;

The Lord shall hold them in derision."

The author may also emphasize his point by stating the opposite in the second line from what he stated in the first in an *antithetic parallelism.* You can usually identify this structure because the second line begins with the words "but" or "nor."

Proverbs 15:1

"A soft answer turns away wrath

6 *Encyclopedic Dictionary of Religion*, Corpus Publications, Washington DC 1979, 2873

But a harsh word stirs up anger."

The author may use a second or third stitch in the restatement in order to clarify or complete the thought he wrote in the first line. This is *synthetic parallelism.*

Psalm 49:16-17

"Do not be afraid when one become rich,

When the glory of his house is increased

Fore when he dies he shall carry nothing away;

His glory shall not descend after him."

Climatic parallelism is when the author expresses the end result in the second line from his actions which he stated in the first.

Psalm 32:5b

"I said, "I will confess my transgression to the LORD,"

And You forgave the iniquity of my sin."

Finally, *emblematic parallelism* is built upon a figure of speech. Generally one line is figurative, the other literal. This form is also usually synonymous since the second line describes the same thing as the first.7

Psalm 42:5

---

7 T. Norton Sterrett. *How to Understand Your Bible.* Intervarsity Press, Downers Grove, IL 1974 133

"As the deer pants for the water brooks,

So pants my soul for You, O God."

When Poetry is not really Poetry, but it's still called Poetry

Huh??

When you study this particular type of literature, it is important to keep in mind that not all Hebrew Poetry is recorded in Psalms, nor could it be classed a strictly poetry. Nor is it restricted to only what we classify as wisdom literature, which includes Job, Proverbs, Ecclesiastes, Song of Solomon and Lamentations.

Let's take a look at a few examples, and hopefully clear things up.

Judges 14:14

And he said unto them,

Out of the eater came forth meat,

And out of the strong came forth sweetness.

And they could not in three days expound the riddle.

The riddles we pose in our cultural generally do not follow a pattern. For example: What is a hamburger's favorite bed? Answer: A bed of lettuce!

Ezekiel 19:1-3 shows the prophet used this style in recording an allegory.

> *Moreover take thou up a lamentation for the princes of Israel,*
>
> *And say, "What is thy mother?"*
>
> *A lioness: she lay down among lions,*
>
> *she nourished her whelps among young lions.*
>
> *And she brought up one of her whelps:*
>
> *it became a young lion,*
>
> *and it learned to catch the prey; it devoured men."*

Even God has been known to throw out a stitch or two. Take note of His proclamation in Genesis 25:23:

> *"And the Lord said to her:*
>
> *'Two nations are in your womb,*
>
> *Two peoples shall be separated from your body;*
>
> *One people shall be stronger than the other,*
>
> *And the older shall serve the younger.'"*

Songs were also written in this style. Take a look at a part of the Song of Moses in Exodus 15:1b-2.

"I will sing to the LORD, For He has triumphed gloriously!

The horse and its rider He has thrown into the sea!

The LORD is my strength and song,

And He has become my salvation;

He is my God, and I will praise Him;

My Father's God, and I will exalt Him."

The song of Deborah in Judges 5:2-3 (Notice how she made use of the apostrophe...)

"When the leaders lead in Israel,

When the people willingly offer themselves

Bless the Lord!

Hear, O kings!

Give ear, O princes!

I, even I, will sing to the LORD;

I will sing praise to the LORD God of Israel."

This style of writing was very popular with the writers of the Old Testament, so expect to see it often as you journey through its pages.

Guidelines for Interpreting Poetry

So now that you know absolutely way more about Hebrew poetry that you ever wanted to, the question is what to do with it once you've decided to study it. Here are several guidelines to help.

1.   Remember that most poetry is highly figurative. That doesn't mean we throw out our rules regarding literal interpretation. Since the language is figurative, you have to think about what the imagery suggests to arrive at a conclusion.

      Psalm 42:1

      "As the deer pants for the water brooks,

      So pants my soul for You,"

      Give yourself a minute to consider the picture. You have a thirsty deer, perhaps being chased, perhaps during the dry season where water is scarce, looking for refreshment. The writer has set the scene of the longing he has to experience God, just like that thirsty deer is driven to seek water.

2.   Look for clues to help you understand what circumstances the poem may have been written or even give you an idea about when it was written.

      Psalm 42:4

      "For I used to go with the multitude;

I went with them to the house of God,

With the voice of joy and praise,

With a multitude that kept a pilgrim feast."

From this verse, we know the temple in Jerusalem was in existence and the author would often join the people coming to the city to celebrate one of the several yearly feasts in the Jewish calendar.

Psalm 42:6b

"...from the land of Jordan,

And from the heights of Hermon

From the Hill Mizar"

From this verse, the author tells us that he is currently living near Mount Hermon, the location of the head waters of the Jordon River.

Psalm 42:3

"While they continually say to me,

'Where is your God?'"

This verse indicates the author was facing ridicule or persecution for holding on to his beliefs.

These are all clues to help understand the motivation of the author as to why he was writing this particular Psalm.

3. Don't be dogmatic. Rather than "lay down the law" poetry expresses the authors' feelings, and emotional state. He is not attempting to teach doctrine. Although you can use this literature to illustrate spiritual concepts, it should not be used to form the basis of doctrine.

4. Poetry is design for meditation. That doesn't mean you sit in the lotus position chanting the passage over and over again. The idea of mediation is to think about it, study it, pray it, talk about it. Take a walk and think about the words and what the author is attempting to convey from his heart to the paper.

5. Your conclusions should naturally flow from the context of the Psalm or the passage you are studying. You should be able to support your conclusions with other passages of Scripture. As you are studying this passage, can you think of other passages of Scripture which talk about the same concepts?

Putting the Plan into Action

The chart which goes with this lesson is designed to assist you by letting you focus on the things you need to help you in your study. You don't need to start at the top and work your way down. For instance, you probably won't have a title for your study until you are near the end of it. Depending on what you discover, you may go to the historical context by reading what was happening when the piece was written. You may discover additional insight from the cross references you also examine.

Use the chart to study Psalm 42. The passage section is for you to make your general observations. We work to answer the questions who, what, where when why and how.

I'm going to walk you through the process, but I want you to make your own notes as we work together to draw some conclusions about this passage.

First of all, does the Psalm make any mention of the person who wrote it? What is he saying about himself?

We learn the following information:

1. He describes himself as a son of Korah.
2. He reckons his longing for God as a search to quench his thirst. (vs. 1)
3. He desires to experience God and has been unable to do so.(2)
4. His separation from God is very bitter.(3)
5. He remembers the times when he participated in corporate worship of the feast pilgrims. (4)
6. He gives himself a prep talk to continue hoping in God and praising Him.(5)
7. He seems to be in a place of exile. (6)
8. He will remember God where he is now. (6)
9. He is being oppressed by his enemies. (9-10)

Ask these questions as you go over your notes:

1. What is his desire?

2. Why is he unable to seek God?

3. What are his circumstances?

4. How does he lift himself from his despair?

What does he say about other people?

God:

1.   Is to be sought after. (1)
2.   Is a living God. (2)
3.   Is a help for the countenance. (5, 11)
4.   May be pouring out judgment. (7)
5.   He will command His loving kindness during the day. (8)
6.   He gives a song in the night. (9)
7.   He is a rock (9)

As you look at these observations, ask yourself the following questions:

1. What does "countenance" mean?

2. Why did the writer refer to God as the living God?

3. What are the promises the writer claims from God?

4. Why does the writer refer to God as his Rock?

His enemies:

1.   Continually say to him, "Where is your God?"
2.   The reproach or oppress him.

The multitudes:

1.   Went into the House of God with the voice of Joy and praise. (4)
2.   They were pilgrims to the city to observe the feast.

Can you determine what has happened or is happening in this passage?

1. The writer may be in some form of exile. (4, 6)
2. The writer may be experiencing some form of judgment.(7)

Other than this information, all we can determine is the writer is unable to go to Jerusalem. We don't know why this is. So it may not be helpful in studying this psalm.

We also have several locations mentioned in this Psalm.

1.   The house of God (4) – This is a reference to the temple, which was located in Jerusalem.
2.   The land of the Jordan
3.   Mount Hermon
4.   Hill Mazar.

These passages refer to real places. Where are they in relation to Jesrusalem? Can you answer the question if the author is actually where he says he is, or is he likening his spiritual "exile" like a physical one?

Does the passage give a reference to time?

1. When he remembers these things, he pours out his soul. (4)
2. Because the writer was at the temple, we know it was in existence during that period. (4)

3. He is oppressed all day long by his enemies. (10)

You should also be on the look out for repeated words and phrases. For instance, Verses 5 and 11 are repeated. This tells us this Psalm has 2 verses. Are they talking about the same thing? Are they different and how are they Different?

Verses 1-5: Appears to be talking about the longing the writer has to experience the closeness of God. In his time of exile, he remembers being in God's presence in the temple.

Verses 6-11: The writer appears depressed, he remembers the goodness of God and the reason he has to hope in his Rock. As William MacDonald said in *The Believer's Bible Commentary,* "He may not be able to go to the house of God, but he can still remember the God of the house!8"

Now that you have made some observations from the context, can you find any cross references which talk about similar ideas?

For instance:

References about the soul thirsting for God:

"O God, You are my God;

Early will I seek You;

My soul thirsts for You;

My flesh longs for You

In a dry and thirsty land

Where there is no water"

Psalm 63:1

---

8 William MacDonald, *The Believer's Bible Commentary.* Thomas Nelson Publishers, 1989, elect. Ed.

"My soul longs, yes even faints

For the courts of the LORD;

My heart and my flesh cry out for the living God."

Psalm 84:2

"I spread out my hands to You;

My soul longs for You like a thirsty land.

Selah."

Psalm 143:6

"Blessed are those who hunger

and thirst for righteousness,

For they shall be filled."

Matthew 5:6

Do these verses add any insight to what you are studying? Look at the promise Jesus made to those who hunger and thirst after righteousness. How does this compare with what the writer said in 42:7-8?

Take a look at Jeremiah's words in Lamentations 3:22-26.

"Through the LORD's mercies we are not consumed,

Because His compassions fail not.

They are new every morning:

Great is your faithfulness.

"The LORD is my portion," says my soul,

"Therefore I hope in Him!"

The LORD is good to those who wait for Him,

To the soul who seeks Him.

It is good that one should hope and wait quietly

For the salvation of the LORD."

Does this particular passage help to explain the reason why the writer of Psalm 42 chooses to hope in God and continues to praise Him in spite of the circumstances he finds himself in?

As you examine your cross references, they help you to gain greater understanding to the mind of this particular psalmist, his circumstances and his state of mind. Take note of your observations in the section "Answers from other passages."

What are some of the insights you have gained from your study. What is the psalmist attempting to convey in his words? What feelings is he expressing? What is his deepest longing? Record your insight on the chart under "My insight."

With any Bible study, the most important part is asking yourself the question, "What does it mean to me?" What are the principles God is working to reveal to your spirit and how do you respond to them?

Psalm 42 shows many things. It reveals the longing we have to experience God in a personal way. We want to talk with Him, even if it is to tell Him we don't feel Him.

The author tells us that our past experiences and knowledge of God can tide over the bad times. He also shows that in spite of the circumstances we find ourselves in, we can fully place our trust in God. He demonstrates His loving kindness towards us and gives a song to lighten our load in the darkest night

The psalmist reminds him self, and us that God is our Rock. That word for rock can mean a fortress or a stronghold. He is our place of refuge. This is a place of security, trust and hope.

What does this Psalm mean to you?

Wrapping it up!

Studying the poetry of the Bible can be an eye and spirit opening experience if we stopped to consider what the author was saying. In today's world, we are often in too much of a hurry to just sit and think about it or to take the time needed to spend in God's word. God commands us to meditate on his Word. Think about it. Roll it over in your mind. Ponder the significance of what is being said.

A lot of the psalms we know in bits and pieces, as modern songwriters use them as launching pads for the messages they want to convey. However God has His own message He wants to convey to us. In a world of instant messaging, e-mails and wireless communication, God is speaking His heart to us when he said, "Be still, and know that I am God."

In Hot Pusuit

www.ingramcontent.com/pod-product-compliance
Lightning Source LLC
Chambersburg PA
CBHW081510040426
42447CB00013B/3172